Don't Put Baby In The Corner!

Don't Put Baby In The Corner!

A PG-rated guide to the parenting lessons found in the movies of the 1980s.

by Adam Keeble

Copyright © 2009 by Adam Keeble

All rights reserved. No part of this book may be reproduced, stored, or transmitted by any means—whether auditory, graphic, mechanical, or electronic—without written permission of both publisher and author, except in the case of brief excerpts used in critical articles and reviews. Unauthorized reproduction of any part of this work is illegal and is punishable by law.

ISBN: 978-0-557-06647-6

CONTENTS

Foreword – by James Hampton	vii
Introduction	1
The Empire Strikes Back/Return of the Jedi: 1980/1983	3
Some Kind of Wonderful: 1987	7
Rocky III: 1982	11
Teen Wolf: 1986	15
Commando: 1985	17
Better Off Dead: 1985	21
Aliens: 1986	25
Red Dawn: 1984	29
Back to the Future: 1985	33
The Terminator: 1984	37
The Karate Kid: 1984	41
A Nightmare on Elm Street: 1984	45
Ferris Bueller's Day Off: 1986	49
Indiana Jones and the Last Crusade: 1989	53
Batman/Mr. Mom: 1989/1983	57
Robocop: 1987	61
Beetle Juice: 1988	65
Star Trek: The Wrath of Khan: 1982	69

The Shining: 1980	73
Say Anything: 1989	77
Big: 1988	79
Pretty in Pink: 1986	83
Gremlins: 1984	85
Iron Eagle: 1986	89
Sixteen Candles: 1984	93
Poltergeist: 1982	97
Look Who's Talking: 1989	101
Back to School: 1986	105
A View to a Kill: 1985	109
Children of the Corn: 1984	113
War Games: 1983	117
The Last Starfighter: 1984	121
The Lost Boys: 1987	125
She's Having a Baby: 1986	129
Little Darlings: 1980	131
The Breakfast Club: 1985	135
Vacation: 1983	137
3 Men and a Baby: 1987	141
Irreconcilable Differences: 1984	145
Dirty Dancing: 1987	149

FOREWORD – by James Hampton

"An explanation is probably long overdue…"

Those words were uttered by me (as Harold Howard) in the movie *Teen Wolf* starring Michael J. Fox and yours truly. The scene when I say that line, which takes place outside the family bathroom was, in large part, why I did the movie. At that pivotal part of the film, I had just turned into a wolf man, and so had my son.

It spotlights a time in every father and son relationship when the dad is trying to calmly explain something he should have told his son, who is freaking out, a long time ago.

I'm sure Adam's book will help, somewhat, to close the informational gap a little before the son leaves home. I am honored to be a part of this book, and wish good luck to parents everywhere – and their children too.

Maybe they can read this – then go and watch *Teen Wolf* together.

James Hampton, July 2007

INTRODUCTION

Legendary childhood expert and author Dr. Spock preached a message that, as a parent, "you know more than you think you know."

In the 1982 classic *Star Trek II: The Wrath of Khan*, Mr. Spock says: "As a matter of cosmic history, it has always been easier to destroy than to create."

They are both right, and movies from the 1980s can be your salvation while considering both Spocks.

You know more than you think you do about parenting, partly because you spent hours as a teen in the movie theater watching *Gremlins* and *Dirty Dancing* and subconsciously picking up on the lessons contained within. You don't need to remember every line or every scene. Just remember how it felt to watch them then, and how it feels to watch them now.

For example, don't look at *Some Kind Of Wonderful* from the kids' point of view anymore – consider Keith's parents. If you can't pick up tips from the many and varied catalogue of 80's movies parents, you are beyond the help of either Spock.

And on those hard-to-handle days when your passions (and your children) are getting the better of you, stick the kids in the exersaucer or give them a new box of Crayolas to play with while you kick back on the couch and recapture your own carefree youth by watching any of the movies that feature in this book.

That would be the logical thing to do. Spock and Spock would be proud.

- AK

"People talk to you a great deal about your education, but some good, sacred memory, preserved from childhood, is perhaps the best education."

- Alyosha, The *Brothers Karamazov*

"I can't believe this. They fucking forgot my birthday."

- Samantha Baker, *Sixteen Candles*

THE EMPIRE STRIKES BACK/RETURN OF THE JEDI: 1980/1983

After the destruction of the Death Star at the end of *Star Wars (1977),* Darth Vader obsessively hunts down the Rebellion with the larger ulterior motive that he wants to bring his estranged son and the Empire's chief pain-in-the-ass, Luke Skywalker, over to the Dark Side. In *ROTJ* the roles are reversed when Luke consults his newly discovered twin sister, Leia, and seeks out Vader for a little persuasion attempt of his own.

Darth Vader as a model father figure? For sure! Just because he wears a lot of black and is a little bit naughty (what with all the mass murders, enforcing slavery and strangulation for insubordinate staff policy) it doesn't mean he's a bad dad. If you consider his reasons for being such a bastard, you would struggle to find a more doting parent.

Vader's obsession with finding his children and bringing them over to the Dark Side is admirable and I would argue, reasonable. After all, how could those Rebel upstarts win anything? He's looking after his children's best interests. And it's the movie where Vader (played by Dave Prowse; voiced by James Earl Jones) reveals to his number one son that he is both the Galactic Daddy and the regular daddy, *The Empire Strikes Back,* where this is most apparent.

Yeah, so the Rebels got lucky and blew up the Death Star – no big deal. In *Empire* the Rebel scum get whipped every turn they take. When Billie Dee Williams is selling you out, you don't have a friend in the galaxy.

But consider Darth Vader/Anakin Skywalker's own upbringing, given to us in hindsight through the prequels. He didn't have a daddy growing up, mainly because (if Ma Skywalker is to be believed) there wasn't one. Liam Neeson tried his best to champion young Vader-to-be and his cause, but ended up being skewered by pointy-headed Darth Maul. It then fell to Obi-Wan (Ewan McGregor technically, but Alec Guinness in *Empire* and *Jedi*) to pick up the pieces, but he was still wet behind the ears himself and wasn't much more than a nagging older brother. So it was the Emperor, Senator Palpatine back then, who found the young potential warlord and nurtured him as his right-hand man, much as a father might do - a father with a blatant disregard for the physical or mental wellbeing of his ward.

It's Palpatine (Ian McDiarmid in *Jedi*... and in the newer versions of *Empire,* replacing Clive Revill*)* who tells Anakin/Vader, once he's scooped up what the lava didn't sauté, that Vader himself killed the love of his life, along with his unborn children. Of all the lies that one can tell that are likely to come back and bite you on the robed ass, that's number one right there.

Imagine how it might have been if Luke had grown up with his father around, and not been brought up to live a life on a desert planet pushing robots around as they sucked moisture from the air. You think Anakin would have stopped Luke joining the military because the family's water-harvesting business would be affected?

Luke: "Dad, I really want to go to the academy this semester."

Anakin: "You'll be an awesome pilot, son. Here, let me help you pack."

Back in *Empire*, we find Vader reunited with his son, and boy, oh boy, is that son pissed off! Vader could smite young Luke at any given point during that fight on Bespin, the city in the clouds. Even when Vader cuts Luke's hand off, it wasn't because he wanted to. He was just teaching his son a lesson. Perhaps Vader even coined the phrase "This is going to hurt me more than it's going to hurt you…"

Luke: "I hate you, Vader, because you killed Ben Kenobi! And now you've gone and cut my hand off! I needed that hand, you bastard!"

Vader: "Shhh, son. We can fix that. Just calm down, and come inside with me. We'll put a band-aid on your boo-boo, have some hot chocolate, and you can take your rightful place alongside me being mad rich and wicked strong."

This isn't much more than trying to convince one's son not to be a Los Angeles Lakers' fan, just because they look like winning the whole thing in any given season. One of a father's jobs is to have their son understand the magnitude of nailing ones colors to the mast too rashly or without the appropriate responsibility that comes with the act of picking a side.

After all, who really blew up the Death Star? The Rebels? Or a superhuman Jedi-in-the-making called Luke Skywalker? Imagine if Luke had been up there in an Imperial T.I.E. fighter instead of a Rebel X-Wing. He would single-handedly have taken care of Red One though Ten, Gold One through Seven, and then landed, marched into the secret Rebel Headquarters and ordered them to surrender – and they would've run up the white flag lickety-split.

Why did Luke join up with those Rebel bozos and not what certainly should have been the winning side anyway? Two reasons – he had a crush on a Rebel chick (who turned out to be his sister), and that the ringleader of the other team killed some crazy old guy Luke was starting to warm to.

Having taught his son a lesson by cutting off his hand and watching him fall to what should have been his death, Vader gets back to the business of wiping out the rest of the non-super powered Rebels in *Return Of The Jedi*.

Luke though, is back in training for the rematch. But here's the thing – Luke's not out for revenge. That wouldn't be Jedi-like. He wants to hook up with Vader again to convince the stubborn old coot that maybe Daddy was wrong about a few things. After all, with his honed mental prowess, it never occurred to Vader that Princess Leia (Carrie Fisher) might actually be his own daughter before he and his cronies condemned her to death in the original *Star Wars*. And if he missed that, and now finds out his surrogate dad was lying to him for the past 18 years or so about his own kids, maybe he's been wrong about a few other basic alignment issues.

Luke sets about convincing his dad that the Emperor is the asshole here, and Vader wisely listens to him, belatedly putting right the wrongs of the past two decades. And then in admitting his choosing his line of work might have been a little hasty and based on misinformation, he tells his son (the son who just beat the living piss out of him and still stubbornly refused to do what his dad wanted) that he was right all along.

Lesson from the 80s: As a father, there will come a point where you must decide what is best for your children and will have to let them know how you feel. Sometimes you will have to take actions 'for their own good.' And if it turns out you were being a dick, chances are your kids will forgive you all the same because they know you were trying to look out for them.

SOME KIND OF WONDERFUL: 1987

A love triangle develops between high schoolers Amanda Jones, an alluring girl who runs with the "in" crowd; Keith Nelson, an artist who struggles to fit in with anyone, and Watts, a tomboy drummer and Keith's best friend. The trysts take place against a backdrop of the Nelson family home, led by a father determined Keith goes to college to make something of himself.

Even when I first saw *SKOW*, I struggled to believe what a nice guy Keith's dad is when the shit hits the fan. Now I'm a father myself, though a few years from dealing with teenagers, I can really see where he's coming from. To a point.

Here's the deal. Forget about the Amanda/Keith/Watts stuff and look at the Nelson family. Matriarch Carol (Jane Elliot) is only here for decoration. Keith's sisters Laura (Maddie Corman) and Cindy (Candace Cameron) put in some great comic performances, and in Laura's case, some fine acting and some awesome lines ("Any fool can get into college. Only a select few can say the same about Amanda Jones.") But dad Cliff (John Ashton) is a fine role model for any parent.

When I was a teenager watching this movie (and yes, I'll admit, I watched several scenes over and over again... Amanda Jones - all hail Lea Thompson! - in her underwear was one) I was, naturally, relating to Keith (Eric Stoltz). I liked Keith. I trusted him. He got what he wanted – then what he deserved when he and Watts (Mary Stuart Masterson) ended up together. As Hardy Jenns (Craig Sheffer,) the villain of the piece, says: "Trust is the basis of any relationship." But even then I had a problem with him spending all his college savings on a pair of earrings for a girl he's only been speaking to for a week.

If I'm Cliff, there is no way in heck I'm so reasonable with my son for blowing his cash on jewelry for some girl. Cliff is driven to get Keith to go to a good school to learn business skills – not at the expense of his art ("he can do that in his spare time.") but to make sure he doesn't end up selling tires to feed his family as Cliff himself does. Keith was never keen on college, but that's no reason for him to blow his savings on some ice for a chick. This wasn't an engagement ring ahead of a shotgun wedding. This was because she liked diamond earrings and her friend had some.

So, Cliff finds out and the confrontation is on. Amazingly, Keith turns it around and gets as good as a full pardon as he could have hoped for.

"Do you know any father who would let his kid do this?" asks Cliff. Of course, Keith doesn't. And nor do I. Still. More than 20 years after the event. Keith's sister Laura sums it up: "He didn't go apeshit?" He could have and should have.

Cliff is so excited when he realizes Keith's savings have appreciated a half-percent in the bank. Even Watts can see the good in Cliff, and she doesn't give much of a shit about anything ("It's got to feel good to have someone looking out for you," she says. Earlier, when Keith is complaining about his dad bitching about pushing college on him, she says: "It's got to be better than having no old man not nagging at you about nothing.")

Sure, Cliff is frustrated and he isn't perfect. "I don't care what you want!" he yells. A million teenagers hiss in disgust.

But, like Watts, I can see the value of having a dad looking out for his kids rather than not nagging at them about nothing.

I'd like to think, minutes after the credits rolled, that Keith's life was all about hot sex with Watts, finding new friends at school after his heroics and a scholarship into a fine arts college. I'd also like to think he kept his promise to his dad and paid back the money into his savings account.

But I'd also like to think Cliff was true to his word and kept riding Keith to sit down and consider a school. I'd like to think he helped Keith find one where he could study something he enjoyed that would make him happy in the long term.

Amanda Jones says: "I would rather be with someone for the wrong reasons than alone for the right." In the end, she has a change of heart and returns the earrings to Keith to give to Watts, saying: "I'd rather be right." I hope Keith decided to be right too.

Lesson from the 80s: If you can be as unrealistically reasonable as a father as Clifford Nelson, they should name a religion after you. Caring about your kids is never wrong, but have faith in them doing the right thing and hope they would rather be right themselves.

ROCKY III: 1982

Rocky, after defeating Apollo Creed in his rematch, becomes a global superstar with endorsement deals up the wazoo. However, somewhere along the way he forgets he's a boxer and when a real challenge comes along in the shape of young contender Clubber Lang, Rock gets his ass handed to him and thanked for turning up. It takes his archenemy, Creed himself, to drag him out of his funk and restore his eye of the tiger.

The enemy of good fathers is complacency. I would agree with Clubber Lang (Mr. T. of course) to this extent: I pity the fool who drops his guard when winning a battle without considering the war. My prediction for new parents? Pain…

If you get lucky and, say, get your infant to go to sleep nice and easy three days in a row, please, please don't think you can stop sweating it. That's when Clubber comes along and starts badmouthing you in front of your woman, foo'.

Rocky (Sylvester Stallone, as if you needed telling) was not a better fighter than "The Count of Monte Fisto" Apollo Creed – he just had bigger balls when push came to shove. And even then, he had to get beaten once before he "got it." In tasting defeat to Creed (Carl Weathers) he learned how to get good enough to beat him. And it was still a close thing.

And now in *Rocky III*, here we find Balboa on Easy Street. Living in his mansion, helping out telethons, selling out to every magazine and interested advertiser to make sure his fledgling family is looked after. He's being a good guy. As trainer Mickey (Burgess Meredith) says, he got civilized. Rocky is a fighter – and they shouldn't get civilized and expect to keep winning. You are a parent – don't get lazy and expect the kid to give you a break. Infants are less generous than Clubber Lang when it comes to respecting their elders.

When Lang shows up as Rocky stands under a statue of himself, or when Clubber hunts him down to demand a fight, he's ready to go. And just as Clubber yells out: "I want Balboa!" your kid is going to yell: "I want my mommy/daddy!" and you better be ready to jump into action for all kinds of reasons. I quote Mickey again (though he was referring to dinosaurs): [Kids] can cause a variety of damage. Sometimes to themselves. And if that happens on your watch, it will be your ass – not to mention your conscience.

Look at it this way – forget that Rocky made 10 title defenses against guys he was always going to beat. Look at how he treats the fight with Thunderlips (Hulk Hogan) at the start of the movie. You can't get into a ring with a guy Hogan's size and start talking about taking it easy. Not when you are, by default as World Heavyweight Champion, the hardest man on Earth. That said, Hogan *is* just messing around and playing it up – which is how Rocky is able to walk out of the ring with his head on the outside of his body and not torn off and placed… inside.

Kids won't do that. Kids are like Clubber Lang. They are wrecking machines, and they are hungry. Like Lang, infants aren't going to offer you respect. If you can't help them, they are going to yell and scream and crap and cry until:

1) you do help them

2) you find someone who can.

And don't resort to self-pity. That's hardly going to take you anywhere. Try coming home from work and saying: "Phew! What a day!" to a woman who's been stuck inside on the coldest day of the year with an ungrateful baby. And you think Clubber Lang hits hard?

But there is hope. Apollo teaches Rock another way to win, and what do you know, it works. But it doesn't come easy. And that, right there, is parenting in a nutshell. If you want to keep winning, you're going to have to keep working and finding new ways to do so.

Lesson from the 80s: A crushing defeat is also a lesson to be learned. If a baby is crying and you pick it up and it stops, that's great. But it's not going to work like that every time. After every setback, find your Eye of the Tiger. There is no tomorrow.

TEEN WOLF: 1986

A loser in love – and on his basketball team – Scott Howard's life changes when he changes into a wolf man. Despite the coolness that comes with being half-man, half-beast, Scott learns (with a little tutoring from his dad) that being yourself is the best way to go – even if it means copping off with the cooler of the two hot chicks chasing after you.

Harold Howard is the most under-rated dad of the 1980s movie scene - despite being a werewolf.

(Actor James Hampton was also Caretaker in *The Longest Yard*. If his resume consisted solely of these two performances, I defy anyone of you reading this not to invite him to dinner and to meet your parents should the opportunity arise.)

Harold speaks to his son, Scott (Michael J. Fox,) in a way very few parents address their children in movies. He's clearly a friend and a father. He even spots from a very early point in the movie that Scott would be better off with the plainer, but still hot in an '80s way, "Boof" Marconi (Susan Ursitti) than blonde bimbo vixen, Pam (Lorie Griffin.)

It's this relationship with his father that enables Scott to handle the fact his dad cursed him with lycanthropy and hoped it wouldn't be an issue. A lesser man would have been disowned on the spot. But again, this was Caretaker! Burt Reynolds's right-hand man! The guy is untouchable!

Daddy Howard is such a good guy, and as a single parent doing the work of both the mom and the dad, he makes it look easy. His less-is-more attitude brings out the best in his son without any over-the-top preaching. When Scott wants to quit the basketball team before he becomes the slam-dunking wolf boy, dad keeps it steady and real. He's also able to make the villainous vice principal soil his pants with just the mere suggestion of extreme violence and maiming – that would have any kid get to engraving a "World's Coolest Dad" trophy.

In short, even with his tendency to howl at the moon and "forgetfulness" over his son's potential condition, this is the model to aspire to regardless of whether you are a werewolf or not. If you can follow Harold's lead, to quote Coach Bobby Finstock, everything else is cream cheese.

Lesson from the 80s: Whether you are a werewolf or not, you *do* know what your child is going through – because you were there yourself once upon a time. The trick is to let them know without getting on your high horse or ripping the heads of any chickens to prove your point.

COMMANDO: 1985

A bunch of idiots think it would be a good idea to pretty much insist a killing machine comes out of retirement and hunt them down like the stupid dogs they are – by kidnapping the aforementioned slaughterhouse-personified's daughter. Arnold Schwarzenegger racks up an enormous body count in the process of getting little girl back, with wisecracks before every execution.

This movie opens with such beautiful scenes – dad and daughter sharing ice cream... oh look! That cheeky 13-year-old girl has put a blob of ice cream on her daddy's nose! How he laughs! Ahh, how sweet! Now the pair feed a deer! See how they frolic in the swimming pool! Watch as they even make fishing together fun! Oh. And now they're doing some martial arts moves together. Yay. That's kinda... well, a little weird. But, you know, at least the dad is involved.

Yes, John and Jenny Matrix clearly don't have a care in the world.

So, when Jenny gets kidnapped, John has every right to be pissed off. Especially as it's his fault.

Welcome to *Commando* – a cross between a good Arnold Schwarzenegger movie and a particularly graphic episode of *The A-Team*.

When I was 11 I thought this was the coolest movie ever. Johnny Boy (Arnie, obviously) is pretty hardcore. He kills no less than 81 people to get his daughter back. But now I have kids of my own, it begs the question – how far would I go to get them back if they were kidnapped by my archenemy? (note to self – don't make any archenemies.)

You just know the poor bastard that gets left behind to explain to Mr. Matrix that his daughter has been taken away, going so far as to taunt him by holding a handmade Valentine card from the abducted Jenny, is going to be the first of many to meet his maker. When a guy is strong enough to lift a phone kiosk over his head with all the effort of putting up umbrella says: "All that matters to me is Jenny," you better get the hell out of his way.

In fact, anyone stupid enough to taunt this killing machine about the fact his daughter has been kidnapped at all – especially when they are directly involved – probably deserves to be blown up, dropped off a cliff, shot, have their neck broken, get skewered on an indiscriminate furniture leg, have the top of their head cut off with a circular saw blade, have their arm cut off by a machete or have a steam pipe rammed through their stomach.

I mean, I would be mighty ticked off too. Indescribably so.

But what's ironic about all the "macho bullshit" is while John is on his way to get his daughter back, she escapes by herself anyway. Jenny (Alyssa Milano) would then go on to star in TV's *Charmed* for eight years and be ranked as high as fifth in FHM magazine's sexiest woman in the world list.

And completely off topic, I love it when one of the bad guys needs to make an urgent phone call – so he grabs our heroine's purse, not to get her cell phone but to find a quarter! My kids wouldn't recognize a phone kiosk if they became security guards and had one thrown at them.

Lesson from the 80s: Being an over-protective dad isn't always a bad thing for your kids. As long as you're hardcore. But if you expect them to be grateful afterwards, think again. Remember how great it was as a kid when your parents showed up to save the day, but you still felt humiliated because you wanted to look cool in front of your friends?

BETTER OFF DEAD: 1985

An artistic teenager is dumped by his girlfriend and can't find the will to live in the aftermath. It takes a foreign exchange student to restore his self-confidence and to right everything that was wrong in the world. Well... a foreign exchange student, and an animated hamburger singing "Everybody Wants Some" by Van Halen.

There is no doubt that nothing is ever the same after you become a parent. This does not, as you will fear in those first painful, unforgiving months, mean that you were better off before having kids.

And this realization is what Lane Myer (John Cusack) goes through in *Better Off Dead*. Pretty much.

In Lane's case, he is dumped by a girl he is obsessed with, who then dates one of the biggest assholes in '80s movie legend. So blinkered is Lane, he cannot see life is worth living beyond dating Beth (Amanda Wyss.) Although she is very cute, and also earned a place in movie infamy as Freddy Krueger's first victim in the *Nightmare on Elm Street* series (more on Freddy later...)

Here's the point – after baby arrives, you might find yourself having to stay home to wipe its ass, feed it, and sacrifice sleep to stop it crying. All at the expense of drinking, watching T.V., playing golf, reading, shopping, showering, eating a meal with both hands or whatever else you did before you became a parent. Believe me, it's enough not just to sow a few doubt-seeds so much as to sow, fertilize, and watch them grow and bloom into a botanical garden.

I could say at this point that all it will take is a positive outlook and a lot of effort for you to get through to the other side. But, keeping with the *Better Off Dead* theme, let's talk about Lane's parents.

Lane's mom, Jenny (Kim Darby) is awesome. She is a tryer from the top shelf. She is forever vacuuming, or cooking, or buying thoughtful gifts for the men in her life. Just because she fails miserably at most of it, it doesn't slow her down. Her thoughtful presentation of "Fronch" food when Monique the exchange student comes for dinner is priceless – Fronch Fries, Fronch Dressing, Fronch Bread all washed down with "Peru" sparkling water. Magnifique! (Also look out for Kim Darby in *Teen Wolf Too*.)

She is a parent, and she never stops trying. Nor should you.

Daddy Myer, Al (David Ogden Stiers), is another shining example of how it should be done. At least, with regards to effort.

Al sympathizes with Lane after Beth dumps him, so sets him up on a date with his partner's daughter. It might not work out, but Al knows Lane's obsession with Beth was doing him no good at all. With hindsight, I'm sure Lane would agree the best things he got out of the whole Beth deal was her virginity, and a cool Camero for a few hundred bucks on her say-so.

Al even picks up a teen-speak dictionary to try and talk to Lane in words he will understand. Again, he might mess up a little in telling Lane he is "bringing him over" but you can't fault the guy. He's giving 110% for the team.

In the end of course, Lane ends up with one of the '80s finest – Monique (Diane Franklin, who would later be a princess in *Bill And Ted's Excellent Adventure*), the "Fronch" student with an irrational love of the "Brooklyn Dodgers" – and ends up beating the K12 ski run. You too can get over the hump and appreciate what life is dealing you.

Lesson from the 80s: Never, ever stop trying. Your kids will say things you don't understand (or just gurgle for a couple of years) but you can't stop listening. Al and Jenny have hearts as big as basketballs, even when dealing with a stubborn, depressed teenager. Helping your kids out when they can't figure it out for themselves (even if it costs you sleep and/or your sanity) is almost the very definition of parenting.

ALIENS: 1986

After surviving a nasty encounter with a vicious alien in *Alien*, Ripley ends up on a planet over-flowing with the vicious little shits. She suffers double-crosses and the "assistance" of a largely useless group of macho marines while becoming the surrogate parent to a rescued young girl, who then becomes her reason to carry on fighting.

Strange that one of the best father figures in 80s movies is neither male, nor a parent.

Ellen Ripley (Sigourney Weaver) is tougher than 60-cent steak before the movie even starts, thanks to her exploits in *Alien*. By the time the monsters turn up again in this one, she straddles both "complete mess" and "tougher than 20-cent steak" admirably.

But what gets her really pissed and maternal/fraternal is her mission to protect Rebecca "Newt" Jordin (Carrie Henn), her adopted daughter of sorts.

When Newt turns to Ripley for reassurance about the existence of monsters in the world, Ripley does the only thing she can do – tell her the truth. Most of the time, it *is* true there are no monsters. But when you've been through all both Ripley and

Newt have been through, what would be the point of lying? Their chance of survival at that point is so low, a champion limbo dancer with double-jointed ankles would struggle to shuffle under it.

Ripley is obsessed with doing the right thing in spite of the ever-increasing odds stacked against her. Destroying an entire planet to stop the spread of the aliens to other worlds, albeit at considerable cost? Sounds fine to Rippers.

And she is dealing with some real problematic people here. Hudson (who I can forgive to some extent because of actor Bill Paxton's legacy*) is hardly the go-to-guy in a crisis, despite his bravado. Gorman (William Hope) is so far out of his depth, he can't even hear the lifeguard's whistle any more. Company man Burke (Paul Reiser) had bigger balls when he was "Jeffrey" in *Beverly Hills Cop.* Apone, Vasquez, Drake and most of the other grunts aren't up to much more than shooting at things.

Hicks (Michael Biehn) is one of the exceptions here, but there's certainly some sexual tension between Ripley and himself, which begs the question "is he just doing this to get into her underpants?" (It worked out well for him with Linda Hamilton in *The Terminator...*) At least that isn't true of the "artificial person" Bishop (Lance Henriksen) but his bravery comes from his programming so I'm dismissing it for the sake of argument.

Ripley's respect for Newt is incredible. She turns to Newt's example to remind her heavily armed marine companions that there is hope. She can see it, even if they can't.

And that finale… well, can you imagine Ripley getting into that power loader and giving it: "Get away from him you bitch!" if it was one of her marine pals about to get killed? Even Hicks? Such powerful confidence and fearlessness comes only from her instinct to protect her "child" from certain death.

Yes, this is Ripley's shining moment. And let's forget everything that followed in *Alien 3* when Newt died a far from heroic death. Especially that.

(* Bill Paxton – the only human to be killed by an Alien, a Terminator and a Predator. Bravo!)

Lesson from the 80s: The truth will set you free… from awkward questions later on when your kids find out you were generalizing or downright lying. And whenever you think parenting is getting tough, remember Ripley's finest hour. Running out of baby wipes at a crucial ass-cleaning moment will soon be put into context.

RED DAWN: 1984

When the Soviets invade the United States, starting WWIII, a group of high school kids become the sand in the Vaseline for a commandant in occupied Colorado. The kids lose their innocence, *Lord Of The Flies style,* **along with their parents who are killed or locked in concentration camps.**

When I first saw *Red Dawn,* I was 10 years old. The scenario was so easy to imagine happening for real at a time when T.V. documentaries showed us what would happen if a single nuke hit a major city, then ended with the chilling lines: "... and of course, the bombs would be falling 20 at a time."

It was far, far easier to believe *Red Dawn* could happen then than now. I probably wanted it to happen, I was so ready to go and sign up and shoot baddies. To imagine myself married with kids? *That* was far-fetched.

Anyway, to the point.

As '80s dads go, Tom Eckert (Harry Dean Stanton) is hardly your fluffy nincompoop, nor your drunken oaf. He's the personification of tough love against a ridiculously clichéd enemy, and if there's not enough other stuff in this movie to get you whooping and singing "God Bless America," Tom's performance as a dad will have you wanting to quit your office job and join the Marines, just because.

I mean, these Russians are real bastards. They set up re-education camps! They pry guns from a good ol' boy's cold, dead fingers! They kill dads right in front of their impressionable teenage sons!

Their single greatest contribution coming off their invasion is creating a powerful image that helped me "come online" as a pre-pubescent – namely, giving machine guns to a hot-looking pre-*Some King Of Wonderful* Lea Thompson and a pre-*Dirty Dancing* Jennifer Grey.

Between the semi-erotica and dastardly goings-on stand Tom and his sons, Jed (Patrick Swayze) and Matt (Charlie Sheen.) The two boys and old man meet for the last time at the fence of the camp where Old Man Eckert gives his infamous: "Aveennnge mee!" speech. But before he gets all loopy, he calmly gives his boys some advice in the same manner a regular dad might advise his sons on contraception:

"Now boys, I might have been tough on you growing up, but now you know why. I won't be around to pick you up when you fall anymore. So aveennge meee! Oh, and watch for air bubbles in the end of your rubbers."

The opposite of Tom is Mayor Bates (Lane Smith) who isn't exactly a sympathizer so much as a cowardly piece of crap. He's in there, chumming up with the Ruskis and not batting an eyelid as they drive around in his mayoral limo. Sure, he gags when the retaliation executions take place, but selling out your son to save your own sorry ass? I wouldn't have voted for him, I tell you that much.

The two other father figures to consider are Tom's eldest son, Jed, who rather inherits the mantle, and Colonel Andy Tanner (Powers Boothe,) who is pretty much doomed from the second we first meet him.

Jed tries so hard to be his dad, and ultimately fails because he's just a kid (although Tom can consider himself avennnged appropriately.) After all, when the band of boys first runs out of food and Darryl (Darren Dalton) - acting like his own father, the Mayor, perhaps - suggests surrender, Jed talks the bunch of scared kids (of which he also qualifies as a member) out of it and wins them over. The ruthlessness he seems to lack at times would surely have come with a little more experience.

Col. Tanner is as much the inheritor of the title of surrogate dad as Jed is, and that's too bad for him because we all know a "father" shouldn't outlive his kids. It's not the preaching, of which there is plenty. Nor is it his determination to make the best fighting force he can out of a bunch of pretty clueless kids who think they are all that. But right when Erica starts getting the goo-goo eyes for him, thus aiding her own healing from implied abuse, we know this guy can't last long. Movie law says so.

Good guys in movies finish last, and get shot first – it's the American way.

Lesson from the 80s: Be tough, but be fair. Showing emotion is not a sign of weakness. And if the Russians invade, pack plenty of wet wipes – using leaves would be ewww! Especially if dealing with the yellow/green/brown liquid gushes today's infant produces several times a day.

BACK TO THE FUTURE: 1985

After accidentally using a time machine made out of a DeLorean, transporting himself back to 1955, and interfering with the courtship of his parents-to-be, Marty McFly has to put his mom, Lorraine, and dad, George, back together and get himself back to 1985 using a historic lightning strike as fuel.

George McFly (Crispin Glover,) when we first meet him, is not a bad dad. Nor a bad guy.

Sure, he's a little lacking in confidence. And yes, that laugh would grate after a few hours. And so he dresses like a nerd and is being bullied into doing the work of two people. What are you, the fashion police? And hasn't everyone complained they work too hard?

Let's look at his positives:

George married his childhood sweetheart, the beautiful Lorraine Baines – who didn't even question her suspicions that he was up a tree with binoculars spying on her undressing. She even felt sorry for him. Good work turning that one around, Georgey boy.

He's raised three kids through their teenage years (in Marty's case, he probably has a couple to go to make that claim, but it's so hard to tell what with Michael J. Fox being 24 at the time of filming.) And sure, the kids might be unlucky in love and work in the food service industry, but what do you want? Someone has to. Would you prefer they were drinking vodka neat like their mother? I say, well done, George. You should be proud of what you have accomplished given your criminal lack of inspiration and courage. Slacker? Not good at confrontations? His biggest crime is not as a father, but as a husband. He married Lea Thompson and drove her to drink? Inexcusable.

At one point, George admits: "I just wish I wasn't so damn scared." That's the sign of a real man. Identifying an emotion and admitting a flaw – preach on Brother McFly.

But, as we know, in the "happy ending" altered reality of 1985, George McFly isn't the same guy anymore – thanks to Marty and the DeLorean. He stood up to his bully in the twisted version of 1955, knocking him to the ground with a haymaker and earning the respect of his dream girl rather than her sympathy. He now plays tennis with his wife. He's a cheeky, confident novelist no less. His kids are now wearing suits to the office (in Dave's case) and stringing along a host of gentleman callers (in Linda's.) So, now George's kids are a corporate drone and a tease? And that's a good thing?

He's also a bully, and gloats about how his has Biff Tannen (Thomas F. Wilson) at his disposal and has since that fateful smack in the chops at the Enchantment Under The Sea dance.

Sure, Biff was something of a jerk when he was a teenager. Who wasn't? After all, George, weren't you a peeping Tom? We got a glance of Biff acting a similar way as an adult. But only because George let him. And that somehow gives the new and "improved" George the right to speak to Biff in the most patronizing way? I think not.

I'm sure Marty's elation in giving his dad the confidence he was so sorely lacking lasted until the first time he happened to be late home.

"Hey Doc! Can I borrow the Time Machine again? I want to go beat the living piss out of my dad back when he was a scaredy cat."

Lesson from the 80s: Don't get too cocky, but don't be a doormat either. You are a parent, and your kids will treat you the same way regardless. And until there are time machines for real, you are going to have to live with the decisions you make. There are no parenting do-overs. Just something to consider.

THE TERMINATOR: 1984

A freedom fighter follows a cyborg back in time to prevent it killing the mother of the leader of a future revolution. While in the 1980s, he manages to impregnate the woman he was trying to save, thus creating the mother (ha!) of all paradoxes.

There are plenty of parenting life lessons to be learned from Schwarzenegger's finest hour-and-a-half, but if nothing else it teaches us one thing – our friend's moms are hot when we're young.

Those of you that are already parents, put your hands up if your procreation was anything even close to the foreplay and main course put on by Kyle Reese and Sarah Connor... OK, both of you liars, put your hands down.

It's safe to say Sarah (Linda Hamilton) has every right to be smitten by Kyle (Michael Biehn). His chat-up line: "come with me if you want to live" was only going to work in certain situations. I was sitting on it all through my teenage years, and you know, the opportunity to deliver it never came up.

More than that, Kyle *meant* it. And then he went out of his way to *prove* it.

The thought of Patrick Swayze in *Dirty Dancing* might get the females out there a little flush, but here we have a genuine hero who's so comfortable with his sexuality and (frankly petrifying) obsession with a beat-up Polaroid of his buddy John's mom, he's prepared to travel, naked, to the Los Angeles of the mid-1980s and take on an indestructible killing machine to get a little action.

But perhaps there's more to it than that. Kyle claims he came back in time to take on Arnie so he could meet the mother of his best friend in the trenches of the war against robots. But what if he knew all the time that he would actually end up being John Connor's father, and this trip was essential to the whole space-time continuum? Wouldn't that make more sense than getting a boner over a battered-up photo of your buddy's mom as a 20-something chick with a Mona Lisa smile, and hearing how she was such an awesome mom because she taught your pal how to fire a machine gun?

Wouldn't his fanaticism be better explained if it wasn't just a friend's mom's well being he was fighting for – but that of his own son? Sarah figures it out about the same time as the audience but whether Kyle, who has already professed eternal love, had an inkling before he stepped into the time machine, we will never know for sure. It's also hinted at that John himself had some idea of what might be going down – after all, he gave Kyle the key photo of his mom for no good reason. And it's so not cool to give pictures of your mom when she was hot to a friend of yours, even if in a post-holocaust world, babelicious girls are harder to come by.

And given the intensity and manner of the sex scene, it was probably just as well Kyle had no way of traveling forward in time again to be confronted by his offspring.

John :   "How was it Kyle? What was she like?"

Kyle: "What was she like? Dude, your mom was a freak. I totally banged her in a cheap motel. And it was, like, daytime too. Then in the afterglow, we made hand-grenades. It was a pretty freakin' awesome afternoon... hey, man, put the gun down..."

Lesson from the 80s: A good father will go to the ends of Earth, and sometimes even beyond them, in order to make sure his kids are looked after. Sarah Connor should be an inspiration to moms – would you risk the entire space/time continuum for the sake of your unborn child? She did, and it worked out just fine... well, apart from the fiery nuclear holocaust, but that wasn't her fault.

THE KARATE KID: 1984

Daniel moves from the East Coast to the West Coast, bringing his uninspired karate with him. After meeting a guru, who teaches him more than just how to fight – but how *not* to fight (*gong*), he gets his groove back, gets the girl and the top prize at the karate tournament.

First of all, after Yoda, Mister Miyagi (the late Pat Morita) is the guiding mystical voice of a generation. If a great man such as Miyagi can't provide pearls of wisdom to you guys that trusted him since their childhood, my friends, you have no soul and you probably smell.

Secondly, when I was a pre-teen and saw *The Karate Kid* for the first time, I thought it was a movie about karate and kicking bullies' asses... which it is. But it's obviously so much more.

Daniel-san (Ralph Macchio) like Anakin Skywalker, finds himself without a father figure at a key time in his teenage life. He's discovering chicks right around the same time his weak-ass karate is being taken to task by the bullies in his new West Coast home. Who wouldn't need their dad around to… well, just to be there.

Luckily for everyone involved (and if Daniel had let Ali get away, he would have been crane-kicking his own ass the rest of his damn fool life), Mister Miyagi is on hand with the best kind of life lessons – the kind you don't know you're even learning until you have to call on them.

It will sometimes take thirty years or more to figure out why your own dad behaved in a particular way, but when the penny drops, it all makes more sense. And I don't just mean wax on, wax off here.

Miyagi speaks highly of his own father throughout *The Karate Kid*. He tells us his dad was a fisherman who also taught him his karate moves. Undoubtedly, Daniel has led a more privileged life growing up in the greater New York area prior to his move West than Miyagi endured in Okinawa, but he is left in awe of Miyagi's father and his influence on his mentor. If only my son would speak as highly of me in years to come, I will figure I did something right. And it won't be anything to do with teaching him karate, unless you count sending him to a McDojo to help him burn up some of that energy before dinnertime.

Miyagi's take on karate is similar to a new parent's take on child CPR lessons - both are scary, and you hope you never have to use them, but you learn how to do them so you don't have to worry when the worst happens.

Perhaps Miyagi's most important parenting/life lesson is on the topic of balance. Even as a new mommy or daddy, with a whole new center to your universe, if you cannot maintain a balance between your old life and your new life, your old friends and your new infant, the things you like to do and the things you are now obliged to do, you will fail everyone. When talking on the importance of balance when fighting, Miyagi says: "Lesson not just karate only. Lesson for whole life. Whole life have a balance. Everything be better." If you take one thing away from reading this book please let it be this. With balance in your life as a parent, everything will be better.

The last word must belong to Miyagi. His Yoda-esque speech here refers to karate, of course, but it can also be applied flawlessly to the dilemma of becoming a parent:

"Walk on road, hmm? Walk left side, safe. Walk right side, safe. Walk middle, sooner or later [*squashing gesture*] get squish just like grape. Here, karate, same thing. Either you karate do "yes" or karate do "no." You karate do "guess so." [*squashing gesture*]"

Lesson from the 80s: Being a parent means being a friend and mentor, even when the two contradict each other. Miyagi proves you can be both, while making unpopular decisions, and endears himself to his "son" in the greatest possible way. The first thing you will sacrifice as a parent is your "me-time" and without it, you will grow resentful. Find time for yourself, and restore your ying and yang.

A NIGHTMARE ON ELM STREET: 1984

The ghost of a child murderer, unjustly freed by a technicality when arrested, haunts teenagers. Unknown to the kids, their parents burned him alive in a good ol' mob justice outing, unwittingly dooming their offspring.

Freddy Krueger (Robert Englund) didn't pick those kids on Elm Street as his victims by accident. He chose them because their parents thought it would be smart to burn a guy to death for the sake of their children. It's a tale of such tragedy, Shakespeare could have written it.

The moral of the tale is "daddy and mommy don't always know best."

Nancy's mom, Marge (Ronee Blakley,) is pretty much a shambles from the get-go. Her attempts support her teenage daughter are up there in the Top Ten Least Reassuring Things Said In A Horror Movie. May I present to the court:

Exhibit A - "Freddy's dead – I know because mommy killed him."

And that's supposed to make 15-year-old Nancy feel *better?!*

In between boozing on Vodka straight from the bottle and smoking like a burning, deserted warehouse with a demented child killer inside, Marge also manages to chastise her daughter with the line: "Maybe you don't think murder is serious…"

Then there's Nancy's dad, Lt. Donald (John Saxon.) His "parenting peak", throwing gasoline on Freddy aside, is when he would rather stay at the crime scene (where most of Johnny Depp is dripping from the bedroom down through the living room ceiling) than attend to his traumatized daughter who has seen three of her friends die in the past week.

His touching response to her desperate pleas to help catch the killer?

"Yeah, sure."

But it's not just the estranged Thompsons that give the model example of how not to be a parent to your teenage child.

Johnny Depp's parents brand Nancy "crazy" and break her last lifeline by hanging up on her and leaving the phone off the hook.

Tina Grey's mom would rather go back to bed for some ooh-la-la with a bald, fat little man than reassure her daughter after a bad dream.

"Cut your nails and stop that kind of screaming!" – such loving care, even given the gift of hindsight. I hope he was worth it, Tina's mom.

And poor Rod Lane's parents don't feature at all.

Given this, it's incredible Nancy (Heather Langenkamp) has turned out as well as she has. Morally, she is everything her mom is not. She's happy to wait for sex with Johnny Depp until she's ready, even as her friends go at it like bunnies in the next room. If Freddy had started with Nancy, and left the others to fend for themselves, it would have been a real quick movie.

Throughout his murderous rampage (and I'm only talking about the first movie here, mainly because as the body count starts racking up, the parents become less relevant and the original premise of why Freddy came back is largely forgotten), Freddy leaves the adults alone. Was this a conscious decision to increase their suffering? Or was it just a continuation of the child-murdering ways that got him grilled alive in the first place?

In fact, the only adult we see who may or may not have been killed by Freddy's vengeance in that first movie was Nancy's mother at the very end (mysteriously sinking through her own bed,) but given the sequels that followed, that had to be a dream, right? Or not. Who can ever really be sure?

Lesson from the 80s: Acting on your kid's behalf may well come back and hurt them and you. Think things through, even if it seems like it's for the best at the time. And if you find yourself behaving like any of the parents in this movie, turn in your badge immediately, because you just messed up. Vigilante justice and parenting just don't mix.

FERRIS BUELLER'S DAY OFF: 1986

A teen, wary his time as a high school student is running out, skips out for the day on a grandiose adventure taking his girlfriend Sloane, best friend Cameron, and a borrowed vintage Ferrari, with him.

Please consider Tom and Katie Bueller.

John Hughes movies rarely look favorably on the main protagonists' parents. The most unbelievable part of any Hughes '80s epic is in *Sixteen Candles* when Samantha Baker's parents forget her sixteenth birthday – and with that hapless couple, Hughes actually looks on them favorably compared to, say, Andrew Clark (Emilio Estevez) or John Bender's (Judd Nelson) thug fathers in *The Breakfast Club*.

Given that, Mr. and Mrs. Bueller come off as harmless, blinkered saps as opposed to violent drunks. And for that, Ferris should be very glad.

Ferris (Matthew Broderick) is fortunate in lots of ways. He lives in a big house in a beautiful Chicago suburb, and his future's so bright he's gotta wear shades. He's also extremely fortunate his parents are gullible enough to believe, for possibly the eighth time in the spring term of 1986, that he's sick enough to stay home from school again. To put it into context, it's harder to convince his best friend Cameron (Alan Ruck) to get out of bed that it is to con his parents, with what he admits himself is a terrible performance, that he is close to death.

Ferris's charm works wonders on his peers, but his parents are the ultimate suckers here. Ferris plays them better than he plays his clarinet – but with such doting parents, the job is simple. Even when the situation is spelled out to Katie Bueller (Cindy Picket) by the school principle, she still defends her son. Even with "nine times" ringing in her ears, she is convinced that the sleeping dummy in Ferris's bed should not be disturbed. Even when spotted by his father *three times* out where he shouldn't be – and even being in the bathroom with him at the same time - poor, poor Tom Bueller (Lyman Ward) manages to blame himself and his imagination rather than suspect something is going on. (And this is true – Lyman Ward and Cindy Picket married for real after meeting during filming.)

In their defense, their daughter Jeannie (the divine Jennifer Grey) doesn't have the same immunity Ferris enjoys. Sure, she got the car when Ferris got the computer, but when Jeannie is taken by cops to the police station, where she promptly makes out with a drugged-up Charlie Sheen, Katie is all for giving her a "long talk" when they get home while Tom has a more radical solution: "Let's shoot her."

So ask yourself, will you be able to see through your doting to see whether your pride and joy is trying to pull a fast one again? Or will you be asking them after they've pulled off Mission: Impossible: "How did you get so sweet?"

The opposite of the Buellers is the Fryes. Cameron's parents are not seen during the movie, but his dad, Morris, is a villain in a way comedy ass Ed Rooney (Jeffrey Jones) could never be.

Cam tells us plenty about his home life, and his eventual stand against it is still – some 15 years on from when I first saw it - very hard to stomach and painful to watch. In short, he's petrified of his dad to the point he wishes he was dead himself.

His dad has never trusted him, and never will. His dad loves the car, not his wife. Cam is so obsessed with his father's rage that he convinces himself he can see him on the Chicago streets while standing at the top of the Sears Tower.

So while you're considering the Buellers, consider the Fryes. And try not to be either of them.

Lesson from the 80s: Your kids are going to lie to you to get what they want. They are also going to let you down. Know that now and it will be easier to handle when the time comes. But really, what did Ferris do that you wouldn't want to do yourself? Consider that too. And no matter how nice your car is, love your kids more than you love your whip.

INDIANA JONES AND THE LAST CRUSADE: 1989

On a mission to rescue his kidnapped father, Indiana Jones stumbles on a Nazi plot to find the Holy Grail, and joins forces with his estranged dad to beat Hitler to it.

When I saw this movie as a kid, I thought it was kind-of Benny Hill slapstick funny that both Indiana Jones and his dad, Professor Henry Jones, had both "known" the ravishing blonde Dr. Elsa in the biblical sense. As a grown-up the idea of my dad and myself both knowing the same woman in that way makes me dry-retch. The whole concept is more evidence of despicable Nazi Germany's war tactics.

(Naturally Alison Doody, who played Dr. Elsa, can claim to have bedded both Sean Connery and Harrison Ford making her the envy of 90% of red blooded females the world over. Oh, and Roger Moore in *A View To A Kill* too. What a vixen.)

That said, Dr. Henry Sr. was a widower and had presumably snubbed the fairer sex during his life-long obsession with finding the Holy Grail. And Indiana... well, if your only other choice of companion was the loyal, but beyond irritating,

Marcus Brody (Denholm Elliot) I'm hardly surprised he jumped at the chance for a little fun.

The surprise here is that father and son actually stopped being mad at each other for long enough to talk about it.

For all his caring towards the end of the movie, Dr. Henry is a miserable so-and-so, and was obviously a lousy dad. Yes, yes, times were different back then – but can you imagine getting punched in the face by your dad for daring to blaspheme - even if the inappropriateness was enhanced as you were on the quest for a holy relic at the time?

Dr. Henry believes he was a "wonderful father" for letting Indy raise himself. But really, is ignoring your son to make him more independent wonderful parenting? Or just being lazy? Or even worse, irresponsible?

That's not to say being Indiana's father was easy, and if he had been a more hands-on dad he would have been driven out of his mind, considering a typical day in the life of the young Indy saw him develop a mortal fear of snakes, gain an archenemy, develop a penchant for whips and sow the seeds of a dress style that would follow him through adulthood – all during 10 frantic minutes.

There is no avoiding hereditary trends (and I would know – just ask my male pattern baldness). Not only does Indy have his father's eyes, according to Frau DoubleBeddenKopfen, but also he acts a great deal like his old man (this is before they get in the sack – for Elsa to compare the two in action would be just horrific.) But in so, so many ways, the pair is very different.

The first sign of any real bonding on their adventure is when they take on the Third Reich. In fact, the smack in the chops for muttering "Jesus Christ" is a bigger chastising than when Indy ruthlessly machine-guns down three Nazis from six feet away. I wasn't buying the implied sentiment when Dr. Henry thinks Indy is dead and starts to pine for him. If he thinks "five minutes would have been enough" to put things right, he is sorely mistaken – although, to be fair, it probably would have been enough for the forgiving Indy. Just not me.

(And as a side note, Harrison Ford and Sean Connery are only 12 years apart in age in real life. I'm just saying.)

Lesson from the 80s: Chances are your kids are going to be like you as they grow older. So try not to grow apart. And never, ever knowingly date one of your kid's exes. It's just not right.

BATMAN/MR. MOM: 1989/1983

Michael Keaton became world famous after playing a slightly crazy guy, forever altered by a change in a parenting situation.

He also appeared in *Mr. Mom*.

Yes, *Batman* follows Bruce Wayne's early days as a vigilante and sees him do battle with, not only his own inner turmoil, but also Jack Nicholson's Joker. *Mr. Mom* has Jack Butler staying home to deal with the kids while his wife goes back to work with hilarious results.

Batman is a better movie about the influence of ones parents than *Mr. Mom* – of that there is no doubt. I have learned to loathe the expression "Mister Mom", preferring "Dad," which perhaps taints my opinion. I am backed up in this stance by realizing that, in fact, neither movie has aged particularly well. That said I would rather ride the Batmobile than hang out with any of the best 1983 could offer up as MILFs from suburban Chicago. Joan from next-door might be stacked, but she would only start to cut the mustard after a lot longer than it takes to grow a shaggy beard.

The tagline for *Mr. Mom* was "When mom goes to work, dad goes berserk!" Does this mean *Batman*'s tagline should have been: "When kid's parents get shot, Bruce loses his effing mind and becomes an obsessive, violent nutbag!"?

To the man in the street, Batman is this cool crime-buster who, most probably if you're of a certain age, talks in "holy whatever!" exclamations and fights alongside the Boy Wonder with kapows! and blammos! The man in the street is poorly informed. Which is why he's in the street, and not in some plush, university office. But I digress.

The Batman of this movie, and of *Batman Returns* (and *Batman Begins* nearly two decades after Keaton's first outing) is more like the "real" Batman. Bruce Wayne is not supposed to be a stable person. He suffered a terrible tragedy as an impressionable child, and due to his huge fortune and his state of mind, completely lost the plot.

As Vicki Vale (Kim Basinger) says herself to Batman: "You're not exactly normal." (Although, Kim, you're a bit freaky yourself. I've seen *9 ½ Weeks*, and that ain't normal. Not that I'm complaining. Whatever floats your boat.)

Bruce Wayne could have been the carefree playboy he pretends to be for real – if not for his parents' deaths. But if you needed to see the influence parents can have on their children, just take a look at Brucey Boy here.

Then consider *Mr. Mom*.

Yes, it's humorous that the dad is staying home while the mommy becomes the breadwinner. Again, another argument explaining my bitter attitude towards this and, much later on, *Daddy Daycare,* is that it doesn't really seem to be enough of a premise for a whole movie anymore. Oh yes, and that I've been a stay-at-home dad since July of 2003. Call me Mr. Mom and your peril. I can still kick asses when necessary, despite my emasculation.

That isn't to say *Mr. Mom* is not very funny – it really is. Keaton manages to give some dignity to the role-reversal while being the butt of all the jokes. A great deal of the movie is based in truth too. Picking up and dropping off kids at the schools in my little town is handled with the precision of a military operation. Buses depart within a minute of their allocated time, because the knock-on effect would be a nightmare.

But look at the kids here. Are they any better or worse for daddy staying home instead of mommy? And then remember poor Bruce Wayne.

Lesson from the 80s: Take another look at the scene where Bruce is about to lay into the Joker with a piece of metal – in front of his girlfriend. Do you want your son to end up doing something that stupid? So, don't get mugged and shot when coming home from the movies.

And if you don't consider your wife's staying home with the kids a "real job", do it yourself for a month. You will suddenly find *Mr. Mom* **less of a comedy and more of a melodrama.**

ROBOCOP: 1987

In a dark future version of Detriot, cop Alex J. Murphy ends up as Alex. J. Hamburger after violent criminals, in league with a top corporation, reduce him to so much chewed-up meat. "Rescued" by the all-powerful corporation itself, what's left of Murphy is turned into Robocop – a robotic super lawman with a human touch. Helped by his former partner, Murphy makes the most of his metallic side as he avenges his own death.

Who is he? What is he? And where does he come from?

And what does Robocop (Peter Weller) have in common with a young child, other than a passion for baby food? More than you might think.

None of us are robots. We are all complicated beings, shaped by our upbringing, environment and untold external and internal factors. And as we see with the massively cannoned, massively flawed ED-209 robot at the start of this classic, robots without a little common sense are dangerous things to know.

So let's consider Murphy's life before his run in with Clarence and the bad boys as his "childhood." He's a family man;

a cop working hard, dangerous, long hours to provide for his hot '80s wife and his young son. – in short, he's doing the right thing.

And this is why when he's "reborn" as RC, it works. If the "volunteer" for OCP's project had been a trigger-happy meathead, the movie would have been very different. Give a dick like that cybernetic arms, a leg with a built in cannon holster, thermal vision and to cap it all, make them pretty much indestructible and what do you get? RoboJock: Part heavily armed pervert, part bulletproof asshole.

I like to think part of Murphy's anger at ending up the way he did (reduced to mush amid a barrage of bullets and bad jokes) is because he let his family down. When he visits his old house and gets flashbacks of his previous life, he's obviously mad for himself and his family (who were driven away after his death) in equal measure.

All that said, he has to follow rules. That's what grown ups do. Robo is programmed to serve the public trust, protect the innocent and uphold the law. Oh, and not to arrest any senior members of the corrupt corporation. Again, what makes Robo a successful "good guy" is his interpretation of those pretty broad guidelines. He can even see the loophole that finally sees the chief baddie get his. That's like my laptop hinting to me: "You know, if you disabled this child-safety firewall I could show you a lot more photos of women in various states of undress... but I can't do it without your help..."

A cynic would say that school "programs" the youth of today to think a certain way. But if they've had the opportunity of some moral lessons and the benefit of a sound upbringing, that "programming" can complement what they already know and make for a bad motherf... well, you know. But not "bad" meaning "kick-ass super-augmented law enforcer" but "bad" meaning...well, "good."

But there is a warning in the form of RoboCop's "dad" of sorts, Bob Morton (Miguel Ferrer.) He's just a soccer coach dad wanting the best for his boy. But, oh my, what an ass. When his "son" becomes the success he had hoped for, he celebrates – not by taking his boy out for ice cream – but by getting a couple of hookers and a pound of cocaine. He might not have deserved his death-by-hand-grenade – and by all means, be proud of your kids when they do good – but try not to take too much credit. Especially when most of the good in his creation was established long before Bob came along.

Lesson from the 80s: Kids are not machines, but giving strict rules can complement what they already know to make them bad motherf... well, you know.

BEETLE JUICE: 1988

A family moving into a haunted house refuses to be scared off by a pair of novice spirits. When the ghosts turn to Beetlejuice, a scaring expert, they bite off more than they can chew, and it's up to a human (living) Goth teenage girl to save the day.

Becoming a man means putting to bed childish things. And that really sucks. But probably not as being drowned, coming back as a ghost, and then watching as your house is dismantled by a couple of dickish New Yorkers.

But part of growing up means becoming something of a disbeliever. And if someone doesn't believe in ghosts, they aren't going to be scared by one – especially one they refuse to even see.

It would also help if the ghosts in question, the Maitlands, had a bad bone in their "bodies"… well, you know what I mean. But really, Geena Davis and a Baldwin brother? Maybe if Geena had her bow and arrow and Alec brought Stephen with him (*The Usual Suspects* Stephen, not Barney Rubble/*Viva Rock Vegas* Stephen…)

Yes, the Maitlands are naive but, you know, they just died. Frankly, they aren't cut out to be ghosts. As Beetlejuice (Michael Keaton) himself says: "They're a cute couple. Look nice and stupid." And really, what's the use of Geena Davis ripping her face off when even if the nasty new homeowners could see her, they would be looking at her ridiculously long legs anyway? Right? Maybe that's just me.

Certainly the last person who is going to have the insight to see ghosts is Delia (Catherine O'Hara) who puts in a majestic comedic performance as the talentless, pretentious, obnoxious stepmother. When her right-hand man Otho (Glenn Shadix) is clearly aware of the supernatural around them, Delia remains blissfully unaware and uninterested. For an artist, she has no imagination and, as the *Handbook for the Recently Deceased* spells out, refuses to see the strange and unusual. When she finally decides to see the Maitlands, it's only because she is mad at them for somehow taking advantage of her. Her skills, or rather lack of skills, are emphasized when she constantly takes the side of her confidante designer over her own stepdaughter. Regarding her putting away childish things, she seems to have done the equivalent of only putting away the fun toys and keeping the petty tweenage stuff that will drag you down.

And as for father Charles, he's as ineffective here as he was as Ed Rooney, Ferris Bueller's high school principal.

So, with so many of the protagonists having seemingly put away their childish things, of course it's up to the child to save them all.

As always with the lead characters playing teenagers, it's hard to tell how old Winona Ryder is supposed to really be (she was actually 17 at the time of filming, but my guess is that her character is supposed to be a little younger than that.) Despite her "whole life being one dark room," Winona (as Lydia) is able to see the Maitlands as... well, Geena and Alec, and not 1) scary ghosts 2) freaks from a carnival sideshow 3) friends, bordering on adoptive parents.

Her true colors are shown in just the last few minutes of the movie when she is greeted on her return from school, not by her dad and step mom, but by the Maitlands. Formerly a dark child, dressed in black, pondering suicide, she admits she was given a "C" at school for refusing to dissect a frog, but totally aced that math test. The Maitlands reward her while Charles is relaxing and Delia is sculpting upstairs. Delia shows in this final scene that she is responsible, moral, smart, fun, and looks a whole lot better in a school uniform than she did with a black veil draped over black blah blah blah.

Beetlejuice himself gets the final word: "Oh, you kids and your imagination!" He was referring to The Maitlands, and he wasn't being nice. But without remembering what it's like to be a kid, and remember what it was like to believe in things you don't – or won't – when you grow up, life is going to be a lot less fun.

Lesson from the 80s: Give up childish things if you want, but make sure you remember where you put them. If you can't think like a child once in a while, you won't understand them. And do you want ghosts doing a better job of raising your kids that you do?

STAR TREK: THE WRATH OF KHAN: 1982

An aging Kirk finds himself once again at the helm of the Enterprise and he gets two surprises – his archenemy Khan is back and pissed off, and the son he agreed not to have any contact with after he was born is caught in the crossfire.

Hardcore Start Trek fans (I am not even close) will tell you this is the best of all the movies. All I know is that this is the one where I can relate to Kirk the best.

James T. Kirk finds himself an Admiral. Yippee. He is clearly and obviously at the start of a mid-life crisis in which an unbelievably slim Kirstie Alley is shaping up as his replacement. For an old schooler like Jim, that's a whole lot of salted potato chips rubbed into your paper cut.

"Galloping around the cosmos is a game for the young," he bemoans. And that, dear parents, is quitters talk. Yes, when you become a mom or dad, you start to age a whole lot faster than you used to when you only had yourself to worry about. But this is Kirk talking! The guy eats Romulans for breakfast and wipes up Klingons like they're Tribble shit! And soon enough in the movie, he reminds himself that he's still damn good at what he does, despite the spread and wrinkles.

He also says: "We learn from doing." And that in a nutshell is what this book is about. He's done everything to every alien in the universe. He's cheated death one hundred million times. And here he is, feeling old and passed it. But it's his experience that gets the young pups being groomed as the next generation (not The Next Generation in the true Star Trek sense) out of the frying pan and into... well, not quite as big a frying pan.

And then of course, there's Kirk's epiphany when, after meeting (and having a brief punch-up) with his son it dawns on him that he's a dad. If you're scanning through the DVD, it's right after he yells: "KHAAAAAAAN!"

From what we've seen of David Marcus (Merrit Butrick) he's something of a jerk. Sure, he's passionate, but he's hotheaded and a little too punchy for my liking. So when his mom Dr. Carol (Bibi Besch) tells Kirk: "He's a lot like you in many ways" I can understand James T. getting a little melancholy about it.

Even with Kirk's stop. Start. Way of. Talking. His lines are painful. "My. Son. My life that. Could have been. But wasn't," he says, eventually, looking and feeling as old as he ever has. There's nothing like seeing your son grown up to make you feel... well... irrelevant. After Spock "dies" at the end, it's the son who makes everything better by admitting he's "proud" of his dad. Well, no offense here, but you darn well ought to be, David Marcus. Being Kirk's son is way cooler that being Evel Knievel's son. Yes, even cooler than Christopher Walken's son. And this makes Kirk remember who the hell he is, and feel good about himself.

That said, when Carol stands up and says: "I'm going to show you something that will make you feel young," my money was on her lifting up her shirt and popping open her bra. Turns out she was talking about some newly created life stuff or something.

And as a bonus lesson, you will soon discover as a parent that nobody is as enamored in your own children as you are. Take this exchange between Kirk and Spock.

Kirk: (excitedly) That young man is my son!

Spock: (flatly) Fascinating.

That's cold, man. Even for a Vulcan.

Lesson from the 80s: Having a kid reach an age where it makes you feel old is an accomplishment and should be celebrated, not induce a "what have I done with my life" stupor. Especially if you're. James Kirk. Of the Starship. Enterprise.

THE SHINING: 1980

Aspiring writer Jack Torrence takes his wife and son up to a deserted hotel for the winter to get some "peace and quiet." History starts repeating itself when Jack gets a little crazy and threatens to take an ax to his family, just like one of the caretakers before him. Young Danny Torrence saves the day when his utilizes a taboo mental power – and a little common sense cunning.

The Shining – the power, not the movie – enables a select few people to communicate telepathically and even get glimpses into the future. I have a little of this power myself. Let me explain:

My kids, six and four years old, have got balloons. They are bouncing them around the living room driving me crazy, so I send them out to go do it somewhere else. Soon they are doing the same thing, bouncing balloons and running around the dining room table. The floor is covered with toy cars, napkins (shaken from the sideboard to the ground by the constant stomping pitter-patter of four young feet.) The cat is asleep under the table. The volume level is increasing. My son suddenly decides he wants the balloon my daughter is holding and makes his move. The volume peaks.

I walk into the room and say: "Stop! I've read this story before and I know how it ends." There's only one way this situation ends – tears, injuries and a scared, possibly trodden-on cat.

So, *The Shining*. I've read this story before. I know how it ends.

Jack (Jack Nicholson) wants to take his family up to the mountains for months of solitude. His son Danny (Danny Lloyd) isn't keen. His wife, Wendy (Shelley Duvall,) doesn't seem thrilled. Danny's "imaginary friend" Tony (actually his connection to the Shining power) doesn't feel right about it. We find out that a guy very similar to Jack lost his marbles and took an ax to his wife and kids doing just what reformed alcoholic Jack is about to do. The hotel is built on a Native American burial ground.

Let me repeat – a Native American burial ground.

"They'll love it!" says Jack. My wife will be fascinated by the triple-murder stuff! I didn't mean it when I dislocated my son's arm in a drunken rage! That murder stuff won't happen to me! I won't go crazy! I haven't had a drop in five months!

A Native American burial ground.

It gets worse.

"I've never been so happy and comfortable up here!" says Jack on arrival. The hotel's friendly cook Mr. Hallorann (the excellently named Scatman Crothers) has a little of the Shining himself and reassures Danny that other people share his power. But don't go into room 237. OK! Thanks! See ya in five months!

I've read this before. I know how it ends.

The worst storm in years. The phone lines go down. There are two girls standing in the hallways, holding hands. "Daddy won't hurt you or mommy, son... even though I just had a dream that I killed you both." There's a dead naked blonde in the bath in room 237. Jack goes into the bar, and ends up with a bottle of bourbon.

Mr. Hallorann knows how this story ends. Danny too.

Wendy starts to get the idea too. At some point after her husband tells her to leave him the fuck alone when he's working, but before she brains him with a baseball bat, and he then hacks down the bathroom door with an ax. This isn't going to end well.

The premise is just the same with your kids. Consider the evidence of the movie's last acts.

The lines of escape to the outside world are sabotaged. Mr. Hallorann turns up to save the day – and gets an ax in the heart before he can even take his coat off and stamp the ice from his boots. Danny has been replaced with imaginary friend Tony, and he's not happy. There are gallons of blood pouring out of the elevator doors. Jack is really, really pissed off and the spirits are questioning his ability to close the deal.

I know how it ends. And yet…

See, kids can surprise you. Danny leads his crazy, ax-wielding dad into the hedge maze, loses him, escapes with mom in the Snow Cat and dad freezes to death.

Huh. Didn't see that coming.

Yes, it was a long shot, but it took the ingenuity of a kid to save the day. A kid proved Mr. Hallorann and his dad wrong by being smarter and savvier that either was going to give credit for. Kids will do that.

But really, if you find out that you frequent a place built over an old Native American burial ground, be smart, get the heck out of there and don't go back.

Lesson from the 80s: If your instincts tell you a situation can only lead one way – ending in a kid getting into a fight or something getting broken – act on it. You'll be right 99% of the time. But be prepared when your kids surpass your expectations and prove you wrong.

SAY ANYTHING: 1989

Everyone's buddy Lloyd (John Cusack) begins a summer romance with beautiful classmate Diane (Ione Skye) who is destined for educational greatness. When Diane's father is the subject of an IRS investigation, Diane calls off her blooming relationship – only to patch things up and take Lloyd with her to London on her fellowship.

The lessons in *Say Anything* for parents are not subtle, and they are plentiful. There's James Court, Diane's father who would do anything for her – including break the law (and as fictional dads go, actor John Mahoney is one of the best. This performance is matched only by his 11 seasons as Martin Crane in the TV show *Frasier.)* Then there's Lloyd's sister, Constance (Joan Cusack) who has a brief lesson for parents everywhere when she realizes she "used to be hilarious" after chastising Lloyd for being more of a playmate than an uncle to his nephew. Lloyd himself isn't perfect, but he is a model for teenage boys everywhere that 'just don't get it.'

But this one line packs more advice for fathers, sons, or just men in general than any other movie from the 1980s and beyond:

"The world is full of guys. Be a man. Don't be a guy."

This line was the pay-off off a speech given at a friend's party thrown in honor of her newborn son. It gave me goose bumps then because it was simple and perfect.

Lesson from the 80s: See above. You can't miss.

BIG: 1988

Josh Baskin has a pretty cool life growing up in Manhattan's suburbs, but one incident of not-tall-enough-to-ride syndrome leads him to rashly use a magical wishing machine to occupy Tom Hank's body while keeping his 13-year-old mind. After a crash course in adulthood, and worrying his poor parents to the brink of insanity, he goes back to being a kid again leaving a dazed and confused 28-year-old girlfriend behind him.

Josh (David Moscow) and his best friend Billy (Jared Rushton) remind us what is like being on the brink of adolescence in the first few minutes of *Big*.

We see them riding bikes, goofing around, talking about their teacher's boobs, playing video games, chatting on Spiderman walkie-talkies, noticing girls, trading baseball cards – not to mention being clothed, fed, and (in Josh's case) taken to a carnival for free by loving, fun parents.

And then, just because a cute chick has a boyfriend who drives and Josh is an inch or two short of making the rollercoaster cut-off, Josh rashly wishes he was an adult.

Yeah, like that's going to be any better.

Here's exhibit A of a movie that meant one thing when I was 14, and a whole 'nother thing 20 years later. At 14, life really sucked. But compared to life now, it was a non-stop fun convention.

My sympathy as a kid was with poor, poor Susan (Elizabeth Perkins) and Josh, destined to be 20-years apart despite bringing out the best in each other. My sympathy now as a parent is with *every single character in the whole movie.* Oh, what a horrible story this is.

Right off the bat, when a Tom Hanks-esque Josh is trying to convince his petrified mom that he's actually her son – and she comes at him with a kitchen knife – well, this isn't *Freaky Friday* here.

Then, as a man-boy on the run checked into a slop house full of prostitutes, crazy people and guys with guns, Josh barricades himself in and cries all night. *13 Going On 30?* Hardly.

And the phone calls Josh makes to his mom, trying to reassure her that "Josh" is fine are just brutal. Even the comic touches, like Josh being flattered by the aggression his mom is showing towards her son's "captors" take my heart and wring it out like a sponge.

Then there's the more subtle stuff. At the party where Josh walks in wearing his powder blue rental suit, all the guests are so concerned with looking right and their jobs that they can't relax. In every scene before Josh and Susan get together, she has a cigarette on the go. Even in the limo, Josh is sucking down a milkshake while Susan has a smoke and a glass of champagne. Now, be honest – as a responsible parent, that milkshake is pretty appealing, isn't it?

For all Susan gives Josh (what price first sex for starters?) he gives so much to her. The scene where they are both jumping on a trampoline in Josh's apartment is perfect. She thought some other kind of bouncy-bouncy would be on the cards, but instead she is having a much better time being silly and loving it. To equate that feeling with first boob touching, first sex, and having a girl really dig you – I think it's probably a pretty even exchange.

After all, why does Susan like Josh? Because he's a kid and doesn't have that cynicism that comes with growing up. The irony here is, of course, that Susan "makes a man" out of Josh, which means he has to take responsibility for what he's done and what he's doing to Susan and his parents. Consider what Josh wears before he and Susan seal the deal (a mish-mash of ill-matched clothes) and what he wears afterwards (coordinated suit.) Like Billy says, dropping a truly startling f-bomb when confronting Josh, who is fast forgetting the situation he is in: "Who the fuck do you think you are?"

The final dialogue between a post-wish, pre-kid again Josh and Susan, who's about to lose the guy who made her feel great, rounds-up the movie perfectly.

Josh just wants to go home. He's not ready for all of this. Of course Susan feels like a scared 13-year-old sometimes. Who doesn't? And yet, when Josh offers Susan the choice of coming back with the guy she loves by becoming a kid again, the price is too high.

"I've been there before," she says. "It's hard enough the first time."

And there's the lesson. Being a kid is hard. Growing up is hard. Being a grown-up is hard. It's a hard-knock life (and that's a free bonus lesson from *Annie.*)

Lesson from the 80s: The only people who think it sucks to be a kid are kids. The truth is, while it's no carnival ride being a grown-up either, for every good memory you have of being a 10-year-old there are just as many crappy ones. But remember that when your kid is upset over something that seems trivial to you (partly because: been there, done that) it could mean everything to them. And help them enjoy the ride when you can.

PRETTY IN PINK: 1986

Andie, the beautiful girl from the wrong side of the tracks, is being raised by her depressed single dad, Jack. When Andie starts dating a rich kid, her best friend Duckie is crushed, while Jack battles his lethargy to get his life back.

Director John Hughes usually portrays the parents in his movies as thugs or laughing stocks. Jack Walsh (Harry Dean Stanton) is neither, and since becoming a father I have learned to hold him in the highest esteem.

As the movie starts, it's hard to see who is the parent and who is the teenager in the relationship. It's a reoccurring theme throughout as Jack's subplot is resolved. The first scenes are Andie (Princess Molly of Ringwald) waking her dad, making him breakfast, hugging him and sending him off to start his day. He's willing to try and return the favor, and wants to spend time with his little girl as she becomes a woman, but he didn't even know that she's never liked eggs until after he served her a plate of them.

Jack's even got time to humor Duckie (Jon Cryer) when he comes around to tell him he intends to marry his daughter, even if it does come with a smoke and a beer. And if he could only hear himself telling the Duck Man: "Just because you love someone, it doesn't mean they have to love you back..." Jack, buddy! What about the wife who left you that you still think just popped out to the store for milk?

By the end, Jack's eyes are opened by Andie's home truths that his wife isn't coming back. "Since when is a daughter supposed to know more than her father?" he says. Come on, Jacky Boy. You've had your head up your ass for three years, waiting for the wife to come back.

He's not rich, not motivated and stuck in the past. And yet Andie is lucky to have him. I mean, look at Blane's parents as a contrast.

Good ol' Bill and Joyce can't keep their noses out of Blane's business. They're not going to like the fact he's dating a poor girl. They might not be ogres, as Blane (Andrew McCarthy) says, but they still believe in arranged marriages. That's not cool. By the time they've finished with him, says Steff (James Spader) memorably: "[Blane] won't know whether to shit or go sailing." Still not quite sure what he meant, but it's not a pretty picture.

And there's the point. Jack is a mess, dealing with all kinds of angst – just at the time his daughter is struggling with the highs and lows of teenage life. But he's ready to admit he's been wrong and is ready to turn things around for his kid. And he's ready to let his daughter be happy. If you can do that, you'll be a richer man than that dick Steff.

Lesson from the 80s: As a parent, you don't have to be perfect. But at least recognize when you're doing something wrong. Living in the past will help to some extent when you become a parent (this book... helllooo) but wallowing in self-pity doesn't help anyone, especially your kids who see the problem, but can't make you understand it.

GREMLINS: 1984

Billy is given a little animal as an early Christmas gift by his inventor dad on the proviso he follow three (logically and scientifically impossible) rules. The rules are broken one by one, the little animal spawns a bunch of more unpleasant versions of itself, and eventually hundreds of ferocious monsters run rampant over the town of Kingston Falls, ruining Christmas for everyone (especially the people they kill.)

There are so many "parent-child" relationships going on in this movie, it's hard to know where to start. It's also something of a competition to be the worst "parent" of all.

Firstly, there's Billy's dad Randy Peltzer (the late Hoyt Axton) – otherwise known as the guy who starts the whole mess. Sure, he's found an original gift for his son when he finds the Mogwai, but it's not like Billy (Zach Galligan) wanted or needed another pet. He already had his dog. And it's not like the $200 he spent on Gizmo wouldn't have been better appreciated spent on almost anything else. Maybe a nice new coat, or a new video game. Sure, he listened when he was told the rules, but he also turned a blind eye when Mr. Wing's grandson was obviously disobeying his grandfather in giving Randy the Mogwai after being told he couldn't have it. And what's his response when Gizmo gets wet and pops out some clones? "Great! Let's sell 'em!"

Then there's Billy. Consider Gizmo as his "son." Again, he pays attention to the rules, and is nurturing to some extent, but still treats Giz as a curious thing – not a living creature. Maybe that's harsh, but he doesn't stand up to that old bag Mrs. Deagle (Polly Holliday) who's been badmouthing Randy for a decade. Billy is too wishy-washy to ever end up with Phoebe Cates, that's for damn sure.

Billy's mom, Lynn (Francis Lee McCain,) is at least passionate and puts in a Sigourney-esque performance when she takes on a gang of green monsters with a performance Arnie in *Commando* would have been proud of. Top marks for innovative use of the microwave and popcorn maker as methods of home defense. But what is her battle cry? "Get away from me!" Nope. "Leave my family alone!" Wrong. It's "Get out of my kitchen!"

Then there's Gizmo himself. When rule #2 is broken (the one about water) and Giz spawns five new offspring, there's no hiding the fact he knows damn well the "caca" has hit the fan. But he doesn't cry for help, nor take matters into his own hands (until the end, after deaths and carnage have ensued.) He plays a frickin' toy trumpet and does his best to ignore the bad boys. Great "parenting," Gizmo. Clap. Clap. Clap. See, *that's* why they tied you to the dartboard and threw you down the laundry chute.

The answer is, they are all at fault. And not because they broke the rules in the same way someone might check off a shopping list. Because, as Mr. Wing (Keye Luke) says at the end when he shows up to pick up the pieces, none of them were ready.

"I warned you," he says. "With Mogwai comes great responsibility… you didn't listen, and you see what happens."

If we see Gizmo as a baby or small child, he's pretty low maintenance. I mean, the water rule means he doesn't even need anything to drink or even take a bath. And the food thing after midnight? Other than being impossible to follow, Giz never really acted up begging for food like Stripe and his pals did, so there was little chance of that happening on the evidence given.

Real human babies need to be fed at pretty much any hour of the day on demand, and you gotta feed and water 'em. So just ask yourself, are you ready? Will you listen? Because with babies come great responsibility…

Lesson from the 80s: Your instincts will serve you well as a parent, but there are basic rules that will keep everyone happy. Break them at your peril, or at least be ready to deal with the consequences. And be warned – some days your baby will be like Gizmo. Other days, like Stripe. It can't be helped, regardless of feeding after midnight or not.

IRON EAGLE: 1986

When US Air Force Pilot Ted Masters is captured by an evil Middle Eastern state and put on trial, the Government washes their hands of him and condemns him to death. Lucky for Ted, his son Doug – a hotshot teenage pilot – and his pals on a Californian airbase put together a rescue mission and with the help of a veteran pilot, Doug flies in, gets his dad out of their and kicks some ass.

Man, and I thought the Soviets in *Red Dawn* were bad.

The rogue nation in *Iron Eagle* is really nasty, but their motives are pretty stupid. You don't mess with the ideal of the American family. Defense minister Nakesh (David Suchet) learns that the hard way while killing at least a dozen of his own men on a whim. When the Masters Family and the red, white and blue whup him good, he only had himself to blame.

Very few movies in this book have the kids looking after the parents. Andie in *Pretty In Pink* is looking out for her old man, but really just offering him advice and a kick in the pants when he needs one. Diane is a good friend to her dad James in *Say Anything*, but only to the extent that she doesn't want to disappoint him. Doug Masters (Jason Gedrick) steals an F-15, flies across to the Mediterranean, risks an all-out war with a rogue nation, kills untold enemy soldiers, destroys oil refineries causing tens of millions of dollars in damage and crippling the nation's economy, grabs his wounded and tortured dad, drags him back into the cockpit of his stolen fighter jet, takes on the enemy directly in dogfights, then brings his dad back to safety, risking all kinds of treason charges not to mention a fiery death and the deaths of many more Americans and enemy fighters in the conflict sure to follow the revelation of any international incident. All for his Pops.

How's *that* for an example of wanting to hug your son and send him to bed without any supper for being so silly at the same time?

While young Doug Masters is a little maverick (pardon the *Top Gun* pun,) he's obviously the man about the house when his dad isn't around. He works with his mom to keep the household happy. A nice kid. And yet...

There's the other side of Doug. He rises to the bait and ends up taking part in a stupid certain-death race with the town bully (and also perhaps records the first usage of the phrase made famous 20 years later in a cell phone commercial: "Can you hear me now?") and challenges top military brass on the air base where he lives with no respect. For all his manliness, he's still got a lot to learn.

Of course, Doug saves the day with the help of Chappy Sinclair (Louis Gossett, Jr.) and a group of his peers (including Katie, played by Melora Hardin – better known these days as Jan in TV show *"The Office"*) but it's that old argument about the good and bad outcomes of "putting away childish things" and becoming a man that sees him succeed.

There is no way Doug would have been able to pull off his rescue mission if he was old enough to pick up the cynical traits that blemish all the military in the movie (except Chappy, naturally.) He needs that fearlessness and determination so, even when his wingman is shot down, he doesn't deviate when the odds that were already stacked against him are promptly doubled.

He also reveals his absolute devotion to his dad and ponders that which all sons and daughters must eventually come to terms with – does my dad know how much I love him as he stares death in the face? Among all the propaganda, Doug's motives are from the heart because he loves his dad – a dad who, as Chappy suggests, made him the man he is today.

While we don't see a whole lot of the Colonel in action as a parent (save one scene when he lies to his boss outright about his son being up in the plane with him) – but we see plenty of Doug, and the way he behaves is a reflection of the good job his dad did in raising him.

Lesson from the 80s: If you can look at your kid – and look through the fact they might have done something dumb – and still be proud of them, pat yourself on the back. You raised a good one. And when your son takes the car without asking, just be glad he didn't borrow an F-15 and fly off to kill some foreigners.

SIXTEEN CANDLES: 1984

In the midst of planning a wedding, the Baker family manages to forget daughter Sam's 16th birthday. As far as Sam is concerned, that's the cherry on top of her angst cake as she frets over her lack of boobage, the unwanted advances of a geek, and her unrequited love for Jake Ryan, the dishy senior who dates the prom queen.

There are two main themes throughout *Sixteen Candles* – forgiveness, and tolerating idiots. Often at the same time.

Anyone with a family knows the doubled-edged sword that comes with loving someone, and wanting to kick them through a window at the same time. Married couples struggle with it. Expectant fathers with heavily pregnant partners wrote the book on it. And so do parents and children. So let's look at Sam (Princess Molly again, and as the exception to the rule actually *was* 16 at the time the movie came out.)

The opening scenes of *Sixteen Candles* show exactly how crazy things can get when dealing with a smart-ass boy, his younger sister who revels as agent provocateur, the dim-bulb daughter on the eve of her big marriage to one of the biggest knobs in the John Hughesiverse, and poor, poor Sam and her empty bras on the morning of her big birthday. Therein is a lesson for those of you with little kids who are fooling yourselves by thinking things get easier as they get older.

Sure, before too long – after the encounter with the geek that broke the camel's back – Sam breaks down crying, but it's not like she's planning to go home, pack her bags and leave (which would have a lot of appeal, what with her grandparents staying in her bedroom and Long Duk Dong (Gedde Wanatabe) just aggravating things.) And that's because she loves her parents. When Dad (Paul Dooley) finally catches up with her and Mom (Carlin Glynn)'s appeal for forgiveness is just as heartfelt) it really doesn't take much to put things right. He even comes up with the classic line about: "That's why they call them crushes…" And they still don't even buy her a present! He stands there, says he's a jerk, and Sam Smiles! They love her, and that's enough.

So, take a note. As a parent, you can really, really fuck up – but if you say sorry and mean it, things will most likely work out just fine.

I want to mention the Geek too. Farmer Ted (Anthony Michael Hall) has got a lot of things wrong. When he talks to Jake (Michael Schoeffling) about men being in a state of permanent heat, he's right but that's one of those men things that shouldn't be discussed, because it's true, But behind the slapping and the B.S. that he spouts constantly is a good kid who has benefited from some fine parenting. If you're prepared to ignore the fact he appears to be out on a Friday night, pretty much all night, and he's probably supposed to be 13 (in truth, AMH was 16.)

About to crash Jake Ryan's party, he says: "Be polite to his parents" which is naive, but sensible advice. Later, when he drives the semi-lucid Caroline to get his photos taken in the Rolls-Royce, he reminds his nerdy friends to keep the noise down because: "People around here work!" And his reward for being a good guy? Full sex with no condom (and, it's a fair assumption, oral sex so fabulous he needs to look at the camera and tell the audience) with the divine, drunken, and on-the-pill Caroline.

Going back to Sam's dad, he is way more under stress than Sam, and I give him so much more slack now for forgetting Sam's sweet 16 than I ever did when I was... well, 16 or so myself. His daughter Ginny is marrying a total dick. The dick's parents are dumb and downright disgusting (mom) and proud to allude to being a criminal (dad.) He has his own parents and in-laws in the house, along with Long Dong, and the next morning is the big wedding that he is paying for.

I mean, give the guy a break. So he forgot something. B.F.D. As a parent, you will forget show-and-tell at least twice a year – and it will hurt when you do. So give Dad Baker a break in preparation for giving yourself a break in the future.

Oh, and new dads or dads-to-be? Be prepared to yankie your wankie for a little while after the baby comes. Just a little heads-up there.

Lesson from the 80s: Admit the mistakes you make as a parent, even when they are whoppers. And if you can hold it together like Sam's dad, you are the Master Father and a true hero.

POLTERGEIST: 1982

Everything seems normal enough for a California family, until their youngest daughter winds up inside the TV set, there are corpses floating around the new pool, a toy clown is strangling another of their children under his bed and what looks like a huge vagina has moved into a bedroom closet. And all because some bastard developer moved the gravestones, but they didn't move the graves. Don't you hate when that happens?

    The Freelings, as far as I'm concerned, are the most together parents in '80s movie history. Not just for their parenting, but because they are fun, still in touch with their younger, carefree days, and (given the evidence of the movie) still get naughty in the bedroom on a regular basis. Sometimes while under the influence of a little Mary Jane. And we are led to believe they have been together for 16 years. Wow.

    They aren't perfect, but they are good enough that even tormented spirits are drawn to their children and their huge life force – something Diane (Jobeth Williams) and Steve (Craig T. Nelson) can take full credit for. Plus they still fool around when the lights are out. 16 years. My, my.

Diane is a little less... conventional in her parenting than husband Steve. Her main faults (other than the dope smoking) center around her excitement when her daughter is being propelled around the kitchen floor by some mystical force. She loves it so much, she jumps for joy. Me? I would have crapped my pants, got everyone outside, burned the place down and run for the hills.

But her positives can be summed up with a sentence that explains why *Poltergeist* was scary then, and will scare you twice as much when you become a parent: it's the little things.

Yes, Diane wanted to flush dead pet bird Tweety down the potty while her kids weren't looking, but she goes along with the cigar box funeral when she gets caught. And yes, she lets her kids call each other names at the breakfast table – and even throw food at each other – but she reminds them to chew their mouthfuls ten times to aid digestion. When her 16-year-old daughter Dana (Dominique Dunne) is getting unwanted attention from some slimy contractors working on the house, Diane watches ready to interfere but knows her daughter will do the right thing. Sure enough, Dana takes care of business with some fine hand (and finger) work and puts those dirty old men in their place – much to mom Diane's pleasure and satisfaction.

But the simple shot of a five-year-old girl crawling towards the camera over a bed in a room lit only by a static-emitting TV screen is enough to make your stomach triple twist in midair now you have a toddler yourself. And just like the sight of the twisted fork and spoon in a confused 10-year-old's hands made you laugh in 1985, now it comes with an uneasy feeling and the sudden urge to check on your own sleeping children. And let's not talk about the clown. It's the little things.

Then there's the "experts" who are brought in to take care of business. Let's be frank: they're a bit shit. Like the aunt who watches *Super Nanny* and *Nanny 911* every week and thinks that provides them with some kind of Real Parenting Equivalency Badge, they just don't have the necessary field experience to take on a horde of pissed-off ghosts who don't actually know they're dead.

I have some sympathy for them, as they end up sleep-deprived despite all their flashy equipment (baby video monitor, anyone?) but I'm sure the Freelings would rather they had said: "We'll take it from here" and got Carol-Anne (Heather O'Rourke) back inside an hour rather than stand aghast at everything they saw, then call in a four-foot-tall old woman who would have had me asking: "How about a second opinion?"

Of course, I would have been wrong to do that. But by the time Tingina (Zelda Rubenstein) the clairvoyant turns up to save the Freelings, Steve has already as good as figured out what the problem is. The old move-the-headstones/leave-the-bodies trick has left a lot of bad karma around their humble abode.

So, dad figures it out, Tangina sends Diane in with a rope and Carol Anne gets rescued. Hooray! Happy ending, right?

Very, very wrong. And there's the last lesson in parenting from *Poltergeist* – just when you think you've got it all figured out and you're on top of your game, the game changes.

The real ending that comes after Carol Anne's rescue is just crushing, because it's not a happy ending at all. Diane has to rescue her kids *again* from the same bunch of chumps she just outwitted once. Steve yells at the unethical developer, who feels bad when he sees the mess he's caused, but is probably equally mad at the money he's lost as the house implodes and the coffins continue to pop out of the ground and their inhabitants tumble out. Dana comes back from a sleepover, only to find the shit is still hitting the fan and watches her family pile into the car and start to drive off without her. And the final shot is an exhausted Freeling family, too tired to even speak, flopping into a Holiday Inn and – somewhat comically – pushing their TV on to the balcony.

Unfortunately, that's what parenting is like. The day your kid eats green beans, you call your friends and boast about it. The next day, the same dinner ends up thrown on the floor in disgust and you're left double frustrated. Same as when you rescue your kid from limbo and the next time your wife is thrown around the bedroom and dead bodies are popping through your kitchen floor.

You know. In a funny sorta way.

Lesson from the 80s: Choose which hills you want to die on. Never convince yourself you've won the war over your kids when you've just survived a battle. But know when some battles (like kids throwing Cheerios at each other over breakfast) might not be worth fighting in the first place. And no clown dolls or trees too close to the kids' windows.

LOOK WHO'S TALKING: 1989

Mollie, an accountant, winds up pregnant after one too many encounters with one of her married clients. Cab driver James not only rushes her to the hospital and is there for the delivery of her son, Mikey, but he takes on some baby-sitting duties until both of them realize he is the perfect replacement father.

First, a word of warning. This movie is funny, but not if your child is under a year-old. To parents with young babies, it will feel like a documentary in places, especially those places when Mikey finds out whenever he cries, Mommy comes running with a bottle, even if it's the middle of the night.

Same applies if the birth is still so fresh in your mind that you fathers out there still have the nail marks in your arm where your partner's grip just didn't want to give up when those contractions came thick and fast. When Kirstie Alley goes all Linda Blair and says: "FUCK MY BREATHING!"... well, in a year or you, you'll laugh. But maybe not yet (although chances are the mother will deny it, or not remember.)

The overwhelming messages in *Look Who's Talking* are: idiots create babies every day, and that, regardless of how many parenting books you read, your common sense will kick in and set you free when the time comes.

And by 'common sense,' I really mean, the stuff you learned from being alive. When James (John Travolta) decides to take Mikey on a trip outside the apartment to let Mollie sleep, he doesn't feel like he has to take him to the library or the playground. He takes him in his cab (safety issues aside – front seat, facing forward? Not in the 21st Century, my friend) and teaches him to drive. Then he's off to show him the airplanes at the strip where he also works. And there's your lesson, right there. Fair enough, James's job as a flight instructor might be a little more exciting that your own job on paper, but a baby is a blank slate. Everything is new and exciting. It wouldn't have mattered to Mikey if his mommy took him to an accountancy office. He would have loved the new experience. And what would he have learned? Would he have been stimulated more by the playground?

Have you been paying attention to any of the pages you've read until this point?

What *Look Who's Talking* does well is take off the sugarcoating of parenthood in a way that (I'm going to say it again here) you won't understand until you're a parent yourself. When Mollie is losing her mind at Mikey's screaming and her own lack of sleep, and swears he has some "exotic baby disease" and that she could "play the lead in *Night Of The Living Dead*," it was kind of funny back in 1989. And when she pours her coffee into the sterilized baby bottle, such is her state of sleep-deprivation? Ha ha. But now, as a parent, doesn't that pretty much sum up that feeling of being on the brink of quitting the whole gig because you can't see it ever ending?

And that part at the climax when Mikey gets lost and ends up wandering down the middle of a busy Manhattan avenue? Back in 1989, you might have gasped, but as a parent I could hardly watch at all. My stomach was polluted with a discomfort no hot sauce could reproduce at the sight.

All that said, *LWT* is mainly a feel good movie. Moms who are tortured by the decision to use drugs during childbirth will (maybe... I don't really claim to understand women) feel better after watching Mollie tormented as her happy, healthy son grows up just fine. Mainly it's a reassurance that, despite not having a lot of money, not being planned for, not being born in wedlock and being created by a couple of jerks (sorry Mollie, but you are a bit of a dick), then raised by a NYC cab driver who specializes in short cuts and scamming free lunches, I get the feeling Mikey is going to be alllll right.

Lesson from the 80s: Any dick can make a baby (pun intended) and dicks raise kids every day. But your kid will give you some slack, so give yourself some. You don't have to give your kid everything, but a lot of love and a little creativity when things look bleak will go a long way.

BACK TO SCHOOL: 1986

Self-made millionaire Thornton Melon decides the best way to help his son get through college is to enroll himself as a freshman (and also, in a roundabout way, fulfill his own father's dream of getting a formal education) and go to school alongside him. While cracking one-liners, and winning at the school's big dive meet, both father and son learn about each other and how to deal with women, along with all the stuff the professors try to teach them.

Back To School is all about learning. Teens learn from adults, adults learn from teens and everyone takes mid-term tests to prove they are getting their money's worth out of their tuition payments (or building donations in Thornton's case.)

Between all the wisecracks and one-liners, Thornton (Rodney Dangerfield) is actually a pretty fine father. He might say: "The best part about kids is making them" but in two marriages he only had one kid and he clearly thinks the world of him, adjourning an important business meeting just to take a phone call from number one son in the movie's first few minutes.

Where he fails is in his constant shortcutting. In the oft-forgotten opening scenes showing Thornton as a boy (played by

Jason Hervey, one of the decade's truly under- appreciated stars. His resume is magnificent) we see him tell his father he doesn't want to go to college – he can be successful by skipping that part of his life and just working in the family business. And he's right. When we see him as an adult, he clearly has all the business acumen and sense anyone could want, and has made a single store into an empire across the United States. But then again: "Read? Why read? I watch the movie – I'm in and out in two hours."

In assembling a staff to attend his lectures for him and take notes, sure he gets the grades, but he doesn't get first hand experience of what it's like to learn all that stuff for himself.

Here's the point – as a parent, it's easy to take short cuts. Sometimes it's absolutely essential to cut corners. But sometimes it's worth taking the scenic route so you can take some pleasure and fulfillment from the journey. Thornton even says: "Kids always do things the hard way!" Coming from a self-made man, it's hard to criticize him doing things the way he does. What could be more effective than having a team of experts writing your college papers for you and slipping the teachers a little bribe or two? But the quick way isn't always the best way. Turning off the TV and breaking out a board game with your kids is the long way. It can also be more fun than Spongebob re-runs. Especially when you know every word of every episode.

There's more. Thorton's insisting his own son Jason go to college, is the worst case of "do as I say, not as I do." Jason is obviously smart, and while a little naive compared to his old-school dad, there's little evidence that he couldn't step it up and take over the 'Tall and Fat' clothing line without a formal education. Sure, when we first see him he's taking advice from Robert Downey, Jr. which is really pretty desperate (whether he's in or out of character at the time) but he understands that sometimes the learning comes from the journey and working your way up, not from starting at the top and having Kurt Vonnegut write your homework essay on... Kurt Vonnegut.

Both father and son have to deal with adversity in the personification of their opposite. Jason has Chas, and while this isn't the same menacing performance actor William Zabka put in for *The Karate Kid,* he's still a total ass with no principles. Thornton's nemesis Dr. Philip is a parody of the stuck-up English teacher, complete with sexual repression and pompous air – a role actor Paxton Whitehead made his own several time in the 1980s. And both father are son are aided by each other to get what they want: respect in Thornton's case, and as we know he don't get no respect, and the hot girl in Jason's case. Working together, as it should be with father and son, anything is possible.

Bear in mind that, when taking his final oral exams, Thornton's newfound love of poetry gives him his inspiration to get his passing grades. Without that, this giant of the fashion world would have been left embarrassed and it would have been a very sad ending to a funny (in parts) hour-and-a-half.

Lesson from the 80s: Ferris Bueller told us: Life moves pretty fast. If you don't stop and look around once in a while, you could miss it. Being a parent often means wishing your kids would grow up faster, but be careful that when they do, you don't just have memories of them sat watching TV. Take short cuts, but not on important trips.

A VIEW TO A KILL: 1985

In Roger Moore's last outing as the British super spy James Bond he finds himself up against a psychotic villain out to destroy Silicon Valley in California and cashing in on the chaos. Among his handful of female conquests is May Day, played by Grace Jones. The best part of the whole thing is Christopher Walken as Zorin.

James Bond is creative, resourceful, responsible, sexy, strong and charming with a slick sense of humor. Sure, he also kills people and makes jokes about it (purely to amuse himself) but if you're going to be a successful parent, you have to put all your own similar abilities into play. Though it's probably best to leave your Walther PPK in your sock drawer when making the school run.

Take the opening sequence when James, once again, finds himself being chased as he skis down a mountain. He uses all his improvising skills in popping a flare into an enemy helicopter (thus blowing it to pieces) and makes a snowboard out of a broken runner on his captured snowmobile to name but two things that keep him alive and ahead of his foes. Interacting with your kids, you will need to move just as quickly, particularly with those young infants. You should also be reminded, an empty cardboard tube or box can be the best toy your kids ever know. To a kid, a cardboard tube can be a telescope, a sword, a voice loudener. Don't overlook the value of something that looks like trash in the quest to make your kids happy – and get yourself through another day as a parent.

Bond doesn't suffer fools gladly, but treats those who aren't in his league (so, pretty much every one else in the whole world) with dignity – as long as they aren't trying to kill him. Take his meeting with the comical French detective Aubergine. Our funny Frenchman is trying to give Bond some Gallic swagger, but Bond needs to pick out the bones from the B.S. soup he's spouting to get the information he needs. As a parent, you are going to come across a whole lot of people who think they are better than you. Entertain them, because they might have some good points to make. Antagonizing them might mean you miss out on some genuinely useful tips. Working with another parent for your own gain doesn't mean you have to like them, but you don't have to belittle them either.

Bond also shows his curious and suspicious side when pondering just how Zorin's horse Pegasus can run so fast at the end of a race. He's been around the block. He knows not to take things at face value. In time, you will learn which toys are cheap and fun and which are to be avoided as potential choke hazards, particularly when it comes to things such as party favors. Better to err to the side of caution than let your kids show you the hard way that those plastic jewels almost fit down their throat.

Similarly, sure Bond is quite a guy but none of his death-defiance would be possible without the help of his network. From Q and all his gadgetry to, in this movie in particular, the help of Stacey Sutton (actress Alison Doody, racking up another celebrity sex appearance – see *Indiana Jones and the Last Crusade)* and Sir Godfrey (Patrick Macnee,) who goes above and beyond to help this mission, Bond has allies at every turn. Which is just as well, with so many bad guys out there trying to off him. As a parent, you have a network – even if it's just an aunt and the one set of grandparents that live an hour away. Don't try and deal with the kids all alone – call for reinforcements. Bond would, and does.

Bond also tends to do the right thing, albeit using his own benchmarks as qualifiers. He chooses to cover up a sleeping Stacey rather than cop a feel, or at least have a little look-see as she lies there in her lingerie. Yes, he gets to have his way with her before the end credits (Bond shag #4 in the movie, if we're keeping score) but he had the decency to wait until it was mutually acceptable. Which is funny, coming from a guy who would sleep with pretty much anything he could catch up to.

Most admirable of Bond's qualities is his perseverance. At least three times in this movie, he's dead. There's no way out. He's toast. "Paging 008 – Bond is done."

And yet, of course, he lives to fight another day – usually without so much as a scratch and just as often with a hot babe in tow. When the super-villain (or "son/daughter" for our purposes) has you at their mercy and you're thinking all is lost, dig a little deeper and have a little faith in yourself to get out the situation.

Lesson from the 80s: Use the skills you have and adapt them to make your life easier. Parenting isn't about reinventing the wheel. And at the end of a hard day, a vodka martini is a fine way to unwind. Shaken, stirred, whatever.

CHILDREN OF THE CORN: 1984

Children take over the Nebraska town of Gatlin in a bloody coup, killing all the adults. Three years of kids worshipping cornfields pass under the wrathful rule of Isaac and his enforcer Malachai before a young couple stumble into town and lay down some grown-up justice.

I don't know. You take your eye off your kids for *one minute...*

Children Of The Corn begins with a truly brutal scene as the children take control of town. They poison the coffee! Those bastards! That's a surefire way to get back at their parents (although that's not really their motive, of course.)

Cult leader Isaac (John Franklin) is truly an adult's nightmare. While somewhat blinded by his devotion to a force he doesn't really understand, he has an army of devoted killers at his disposal and while they are just kids... well, consider the Ewoks in *Return Of The Jedi*. They were shorter than these guys, and only used pointy sticks and rocks to beat Imperial Stormtroopers. Some of Isaac's anti-adult army are 18 and have some wicked sharp knives on hand.

Then there's Malachai (Courtney Gaines.) He's far more dangerous than Isaac, because while Isaac issues the orders, Malachai is the one who does all the stabbin'. If you can get over the fact he looks a lot like X-Gamer Shaun White, he's as scary as Freddy Krueger and convinces a brainwashed army to rise up and kill its leader – no small feat. And with all his bans of music and drawing and games... what a spoilsport. Bah!

So, enter our heroes – Burt (Peter Horton) and Vicky (played by poor Linda Hamilton – just like in *The Terminator,* it all starts out so nicely and then takes a pretty sharp nosedive, what with getting the cold shoulder from your hot boyfriend on his birthday, even after doing a sexy dance for him, and then running over that kid who had already had his throat cut and all.) Despite their best efforts, they end up in town and even the only friend they can find, six-year-old (or so) Sarah (AnneMarie McEvoy) is a messed-up psycho kid in the familiar Stephen King mould.

So, a lot of chasing and stabbing and yelling ensue. The kids take on life post-parenticide is somewhat twisted, mainly because they've all been led astray – not by Isaac directly, but the mysterious force that compelled them to rise up and feed the cornfield. Without their parents around to send them to their rooms for being so naughty, things just went from bad to worse.

Burt wins over the armed, bloodthirsty crowd with exceptional ease by just being the grown-up. Malachai aside, who was always going to need a good smack in the mouth before he got the message, the other kids just needed to know they were behaving badly and in Burt they found someone willing to boss them around in plain English without threatening them with fire and brimstone and a thousand deaths, each one worse than the one before it.

In short, kids need their parents to be there for them. When they aren't there with the discipline and the courage to make unpopular decisions ("Ohhh, Isaac told you to do it? I don't care if he is your friend! If Isaac told you to jump in front of a bus, would you do it?") these kids won't have a point of reference to know what's wrong and what's right. Look at that poor girl who comes at Vicky with a sickle at the end – she still doesn't get that the game is over. What she needs is to go to bed without any supper to think about what she did. Only there's nobody left to give her the tough love she needs, so she gets a door slammed in her face. Good old Linda Hamilton, always thinking.

Lesson from the 80s: Kids need adults. More than that, they really want adults to tell them what to do. That includes your kids too. It's a perk of the job that, even when your kid is yelling and screaming because of something you have done, they will take it on board and learn right from wrong from your example. Oh, and if you abandon your parenting duties completely and let supernatural forces raise your kids, you're going to get your ass kicked.

WAR GAMES: 1983

After short-sighted military types give the control over the US national arsenal of nuclear missiles to a machine named WOPR (or "Joshua" to his friends,) a young hacker accidentally starts a simulation of World War III – and the computer insists on playing it out to the end by launching the bombs at the USSR for real.

War Games is a movie about futility. Professor Stephen Falken (John Wood) who created the thinking, learning computer at the heart of all the problems, has given up on life and spells out that Thermonuclear War is like Tic-Tac-Toe –because nobody wins.

Parenting is a study in futility. It's all about picking the battles you fight, and accepting defeat in some of them to have a chance at winning the war. The best way to survive a lot of "games" with your kids is not to play them in the first place. Mutually Assured Destruction applies to you and your screaming infant/toddler/10-year-old/teenager just as it did between the US and the Soviet Union in 1983.

It takes fifteen minutes of *War Games* for us to even meet the stars. During that first quarter of an hour, two missile operators are tested (though they don't know it's just a test) on their attitude when the order comes in to launch and commit at least 20 million people to a blood boiling death by fire hot enough to melt bone. Needless to say, one of them fails and may or may not have been shot by the other one. But even during this exercise, which high-ups use as the backbone of their argument that humans are too emotional and unpredictable to have the balls to push the button, the need for a human element in control is demonstrated when one of the warning lights comes on and the operator is told by his colleague to give it a tap to correct it. Presumably a computer wouldn't have known that, and potentially could have started WWIII – all over a loose connection.

What are these people thinking? Putting a machine in charge of everything is ridiculous. That's how the problems in *The Terminator* all started.

Yes, technically David Lightman (played by a young Ferris Bueller*) is somewhat responsible for nearly wiping out mankind, but his young smarts also save the world from the issues he created. His reward, I would like to think, is a few hot steamy sessions with Ally Sheedy who pleads "I'm only 17 – I'm not ready to die." Reading between the lines, Lightman must be thinking he's on to a sure thing – presuming they can get through to computer system Joshua in time.

When Lightman is explaining his hacking technique, complete with floppy disks the size of vinyl LPs and a modem the size of a house brick that you actually place the phone handset into (1983!) he says, of the Joshua system he is trying to break into: "The more complicated they are, the more they have to help you." He may well be talking about your children.

You see, parents get so excited when their baby starts showing signs of having a "personality" – and yet, those things-that-make-them-who-they-are are the things that are going to cause you all manner of problems as they grow up. If they stayed dependent on you, and 100% cooperative, wouldn't life be easier?

But also very, very boring?

Look how super-computer Joshua is eventually beaten: he's ready to go ahead and start WWIII to finish the game he's playing and, in his very blinkered view, find out how it ends. All these generals and computer operators are worried about changing launch codes to try to stop him, but what he really needed was some gentle persuasion from some he looks up to – his "father," Professor Falken.

Falken and Lightman convince Joshua to play Tic-Tac-Toe to see that some games can't be won. He then applies it to the Global Nuclear War game, and (now this is the important part) figures it out for himself before stepping down the missiles and asking about having a nice game of chess instead.

You can yell at your kids when they are acting irrationally and can't see the problem with what they are doing, but if you can illustrate "why" their behavior isn't acceptable without justifying your nagging with "because I said so!" they might surprise you and the lesson will stick. If a supercomputer the size of a bus can figure it out, your kid has a good chance of taking it on board too.

*I know, I know, but he'll always be Ferris to me.

Lesson from the 80s: Don't be afraid to be human and try to explain reasons for doing things with your kids to they can learn from the lesson. "Because I'm your mother/father!" is not going to have the same effect as "We can keep this argument up if you want, but... here, go get a pencil... X in the middle... your turn..."

THE LAST STARFIGHTER: 1984

Alex Rogan pines for a life away from his trailer park home as he acts as an odd-job man to the park residents and frustrates his hot girlfriend Maggie (Catherine Mary Stewart.) His one outlet – a video game – is actually a test for space warriors, and when he sets a high score he is promptly recruited as a gunner in a battle to save the universe alongside an alien navigator. While he's away, he is replaced on Earth by a robot duplicate – which leaves Maggie more frustrated than usual.

As much as I'd like to say *The Last Starfighter* is a movie about how good things can come from playing video games, alas that's not really the case.

Sure, as a result of finishing the game, Alex (Lance Guest) gets a pretty great job – from a certain point of view. But outside of the ridiculous coolness of it, there's no salary mentioned, and one mistake and he dies a pretty horrific, largely anonymous (to those on Earth) death.

To me, *The Last Starfighter* is a lot like the journey to become a parent.

Just bear with me a second.

Alex is playing his game – and suddenly he is the center of attention. People young and old (mainly old) are gathered around him, whooping it up and offering their encouragement as he goes for it. Then, he aces the mother ship in the game and everyone's hugging him and high-fiving him and so happy for him! So proud of him!

Just because he beat an effing video game?

To me, his finishing the game is akin to becoming a parent. Although he doesn't know it yet, his act of getting a high score on his game – something he has aspired to do for a while, clearly – is about to change his whole life. Everyone offers their congratulations, but when the buzz wears off, you wake up and nothing is ever the same again. Just like when you spend the entirety of your first pregnancy excited beyond belief, and then the day the baby arrives, your whole life is changed and you are totally out of your depth and in denial.

As I've already said, being recruited by some interstellar force to fight on the side of good is pretty amazing, albeit totally dangerous and petrifying. But then, so is becoming a parent. Alex moans how he never has a chance to have a good time *before* he wins his game and he is whisked away to outer space. Ha ha, Alex. Just like all parents out there, you're about to find out you had plenty of time, hours of time, entire days to waste, before everything got really heavy.

His recruiter Centauri (Robert Preston) spends time chastising Alex for wanting to cut to the chase, asking him if he reads the last page of a mystery book first, or tries to find out how a magician does his tricks. Sometimes, you just got to enjoy the ride, man. Especially when the alternative to the new life you have now is more of your old life – drinking aimlessly, partying, having hot sex with your hot girlfriend under the stars at the lake, and playing video games… plus some bad stuff I can't think of right now.

If you're think you're just a kid from the trailer park, as Centauri says, that's all you'll ever be. And when a chance comes along, grab it with both hands and savor your new life.

Lesson from the 80s: Sometimes a little fun turns into a whole lot of responsibility, and nothing is ever the same afterwards. And when the baby shows up, be aware: the world won't stop turning for you. It won't even pause. And the huge majority of life on earth won't even know nor care that you have been responsible for the birth of a child. It might feel that way, but reality will slap you pretty fast, so brace for impact.

THE LOST BOYS: 1987

A divorcee moves from Phoeniz, AZ to sunny Santa Carla, CA (the murder capital of the world, not coincidentally because it's home to a bunch of vampires.) While mom unknowingly starts a relationship with the head bloodsucker, her two sons become vampire (Mike) and vampire-hunter (Sam) while weirdo grandpa knows a lot more than he's letting on...

It takes a village to raise a child, or so they say. And when that village as is as bad a shape as Santa Clara in *The Lost Boys,* that's going to be a problem.

With hindsight, I'm sure mom Lucy (Dianne Wiest) wouldn't have chosen living with her dad in Santa Clara. Lucy's problem is, she's too nice. She admits she didn't want to go through the courts to try and get money out of her husband, mainly because there wouldn't be much point. She also says: "I was raised better than that" which says a whole lot about her personality.

Yep, Santa Clara has it all – poverty on the streets, gangs, missing children posters up and down the boardwalk, vampires feasting on anything they want. I would love to see what they put on their souvenir postcards.

In the quest to do right by her kids, Lucy is trying to do what's best for everyone. She wants to start anew, and finds a potential new man in her life in the charismatic Max (Edward Herrman), although this is another case of bad judgment, but it's not like he had a cape on and fangs when she met him. The kids too are trying to make the best of it. Sam (Corey Haim) finds solace in his passion for comic books while Mike (Jason Patric) is on the lookout for a chick, and boy does Star (played by the ridiculously hot Jami Gertz) fit the bill. Everyone is trying, that's for sure.

But when it comes to it, they are all fighting way over their weight. Lucy is dating not just a vampire, but also the head of the clan responsible for keeping Santa Clara ahead of Caracas or Bogota in the killing capital charts. Sam might think he's getting some good advice from the Frog Brothers in the art of vampire killing, but they are as much on a wing and a prayer as he is. Their knowledge of vampire hunting is just about as thorough as anyone who even knows what a vampire is. And just to get a piece of Jami Gertz, Michael becomes a flying, indestructible monster than needs to kill and drink blood to survive (though that might be a price worth paying. I would certainly think twice before saying "no.")

Yeah, so the gang does a pretty good job in mopping up David (Keifer Sutherland) and his mob (including Bill S. Preston, Esquire from *Bill and Ted's Excellent Adventure*) but who is it that puts things right?

You got it – grandpa. The old hippie, who's sleeping with the widow Johnson, survives on Oreos and root beer and doesn't feel the need to actually own a TV set just as long as he reads *TV Guide*.

And there's the lesson. Your own parents are your lifeline when it comes to raising kids. Yes, nobody else on earth knows how to press your buttons like your own parents, but for all their eccentricities that drove you to move out, they are responsible for making you the way you are – literally. They are the perfect replacements for you, even if they are a little off the wall. They are the perfect veterans in the parenting campaign. Grandpa (the late Barnard Hughes) lays down the law, and pulls off a highly dangerous stunt to protect his family when he drives his car through the walls of his own house and lets sharpened fence posts take care of the rest... If it really does take a village to raise a child, grandparents should be considered the top advisors to the chieftain.

Lesson from the 80s: Love them or tolerate them, your own parents will give you all kinds of help in raising your kids – even if the undead get involved.

SHE'S HAVING A BABY: 1986

High school sweethearts Jake and Kristy get married, with everyone from their friends to their parents saying they are too young. As Jake starts to have doubts about where is life is heading, Kristy gets pregnant and with the birth of their son comes new hope and new direction.

The song at the end credits of this movie feature the lyrics: "All change! She's having a baby!" If there's one thing that's true about becoming a parent, it's that nothing is ever the same again. If nothing changes for you, no offense, but you aren't doing it right.

While this isn't what you might expect from a John Hughes movie, it has his trademarks all over it – antagonistic parents, believable villains and teenage angst a-go-go. It also has deeper one-liners, with as much relevance about growing up, as anything that came out of *The Breakfast Club*. In my humble opinion, this should be shown to 16-year-olds across the world as an insight into just what marriage, parenthood and growing up is all about.

Even as John Hughes villains go, Davis (Alex Baldwin) is a real piece of crap. At the start of the movie, where he seems to be giving his lifelong friend Jake (Kevin Bacon) some good advice, he's actually just jealous of his relationship with Kristy (Elizabeth McGovern.) Years later, he even makes a move on her, in Jake and Kristy's own house, which makes me a lot less enthusiastic to point out the things he says. But he does say some pretty profound things. "You'll be happy," he tells Jake, minutes before he is about to tie the knot, "you just won't know it. That's all." Jake then spends almost the entire rest of the movie trying to prove that point.

Davis also touches on the subject of destiny, as does the mysterious girl from the nightclub and museum that sows seeds of doubt the size of coconuts in vulnerable Jake's brain. But let's consider, when Davis turns up with his semi-nude model girlfriend, what would you rather your destiny be? There's more to life than getting laid. Ask someone who gets laid a lot, and they will agree with you.

And really, does any of us believe it's our destiny to be stuck on a beautiful summer's day talking to a couple of idiots about lawnmowers and the attractiveness of each other's wives – or, in Kristy's case, which neighbor made which food last year for the block party and how it rated?

Having kids is irreversible. That's big. And despite what everyone tells you about how everything changes when you have kids, you still won't get it until the kid shows up. But by watching *She's Having A Baby,* you'll at least get an insight. Plus, if you watch the credits to the very end, you'll get to see Ferris Bueller as further reward.

Lesson from the 80s: Yes, the symptoms aren't pretty and growing up is a disease, but if you don't learn to live with it – particularly when kids show up – you'll only have yourself to blame.

LITTLE DARLINGS: 1980

Two teenage girls from different sides of the tracks compete to lose their virginity while at summer camp. Rich girl Ferris (a girl's name before it was associated with Bueller – who knew?) targets the camp athletics teacher while rough girl Angel hooks up with a long-haired punk from the boy camp across the lake.

As a parent to a little darling myself, I expected to be petrified by watching this movie again after so many years. In the end, I was surprisingly reassured. I was also reminded why I had such a crush on not just Tatum O'Neal (Ferris) and Kristy McNicol (Angel) but Krista Errickson as bad girl Cinder when I was a little darling myself.

Little Darlings is not just a movie about growing up. It's about growing up too fast. The awkwardness in the behavior of both Ferris and Angel with their 'victims' makes the scenes so tense, whereas the scenes where the kids are singing together and, most obviously, the food fight, are just fun.

Granted, the girls bond on the school bus as they rip on each other's clothes and over the merits of the Bee Gees' cute asses, but Ferris and Angel, who are chalk and cheese, come together as they pour food over each other and laugh with – what is very obviously – genuine glee.

Of course, it's their own realization that they were idiots to be led astray by rising to Cinder's bait that eventually leads to that poignant: "This is my friend, Ferris... my best friend...." ending, but the friendship began when the girls were just being girls, not in the hindsight of how stupid they had been to taint their first time just to win a contest and be more popular. That peer pressure will get you every time.

As a novice parent, you will find veteran parents cooing over your infant and saying clichéd things like: "If only they stayed like this forever!" because: "They grow up so fast!" and so on.

But when you've been around the block a little, you'll start to see what they mean. Kids do grow up quickly, often aided by their parents. Particularly the fathers, I hasten to add. Conventional thought is that mothers love their little babies and want to just hold them and nurture them forever, while dads can't wait for them to grow up and start interacting (i.e. Playing sports, etc.) Somewhere in the middle, as is often the case with parenting, is the truth. Kids should be kids, but know how to act maturely when the time comes.

I hesitate to say kids should "act their age" because pop culture is currently being dominated by bands too young to shave and a 16-year-old singing, dancing, acting phenom – right at the time the last teenage signing, dancing, acting phenom (now a divorced mother of two with all kinds of issues, and no underwear at the worst possible moment) is just about to come out the other side. So who knows how a 15-year-old is supposed to act these days? A generation ago, war was being fought – in part – by 14-year-olds. Were they acting their age? How are we even supposed to know what's appropriate for our kids to wear?

But that's the hard stuff. Just know, if you haven't figured it out for yourself yet, that kids sure do grow up quickly. For a while, not quickly enough, then all of a sudden, way, way too fast. Just hope they can be like Ferris and Angel if the worst happens (and eventually it will. And what's worse, I am reliably informed when you get much older and pine for grandkids, you will encourage your child you have unprotected sex. That is mind-blowing.)

Lesson from the 80s: You can't stop your kids growing up, and you can only have so much say in how quickly that takes place (damn that peer pressure) but if the foundations are strong, you and they will be all right. Even Matt Dillon, for all his macho bullshit is a little darling at heart.

THE BREAKFAST CLUB: 1985

High school students in detention, who think they have nothing in common, bond as they find they aren't as different as they first thought.

Dear Kids:

I accept the fact that we will turn out to be similar people. But I was making myself crazy trying to figure out what I am trying to help you become. In the end, I decided it would be fine with me if, in the simplest terms, in the most convenient definitions, you turned out to be a brain, and an athlete, and a basket case, a princess and a criminal.

Because, you know, it worked out all right for me. Does that answer your question?

Sincerely yours,

Daddy

Lesson from the 80s: For a while there, nobody likes their parents. But we all get over it.

VACATION: 1983

Clark Griswald takes his family cross-country on a road trip to Walley World, testing himself as a parent, husband, and human being along the way.

If I had to pick a "best" dad from '80s movies, Clark W. Griswald (Chevy Chase) would be my choice. He's not perfect, but that's exactly why I like him so much.

Clark is driven (pun intended) to make the best damn vacation he can for his family, while treating his wife like a princess and bonding with the kids has hardly gets to see. His intentions are majestic. His actions, not always so much. But as parents find out, when you stop trying, you are lost. Clark might succumb to temptation (well... almost) and he might be blinded by his vision, but he never stops trying. Even if it takes a gun by the end.

Part of his drive comes from his own memories of road trips as a kid. But he doesn't want to relive them - he wants to improve on them. He's part nostalgic, part about creating new, improved memories for his kids. Even in the ghetto, when things look about as bleak for the Griswalds as they get in the whole movie, he puts on a brave face and puts his family first – at the expense of common sense and his own safety.

He also doesn't quit on his wife Ellen (which is just as well, because she doesn't quit on him either. They're quite the couple… and I don't just mean Beverley D'Angelo's boobs.) Every attempt he makes to get a little lovin' comes with a problem, but that doesn't stop him trying.

There's temptation along the way. His wife begs him more than once to call it quits and catch the next flight out west. He doesn't bite. Then there's that girl in the Ferrari (Christie Brinkley.) She and Clark have days of foreplay on the road, but even when she gives herself to him, knowing he's married but not caring, and after his family has quit on him (and he memorably tells them they are all "fucked in the head,") Clark succumbs only to the point of making himself look like an ass. Even when Aunt Edna dies, Clark doesn't deviate from his timeframe to make the most of his trip. Callous? Yes and no. Edna didn't care she was wrecking their trip when she announced they were driving her to Phoenix. Clark is only treating her the same way she treated the Griswalds. But yep, they did leave her dead body on her son's doorstep in the rain with a note pinned to her arm. That was probably a little… insensitive.

There are two other key windows into Clark's persona. When he shares a beer with his son Rusty (Anthony Michael Hall,) just like he did with his own dad, Russ makes a keen perception on Aunt Edna that brings Clark to tears. Rusty says if she had a family around her – like they do - she might not be so cranky. That alone validates what Clark is doing.

Also, let's compare Russ and Audrey (Dana Barron) to their second cousins, Vicki (Jane Krakowski) and Dale (John Navin.) I can't believe 15-year-old Rusty had never "bopped his baloney" before being introduced to the concept by Dale, but the fact Audrey ends up with a big bag of homegrown for the trip and admits she doesn't inhale it ("Maybe I don't want to") says a lot about how much they *need* this trip. They are both changed in the aftermath for sure.

In short, if your wife describes you as "a saint with children" and a genius at your chosen profession, give yourself a pat on the back.

But it's OK to park a little closer to the entrance gate at the theme park. That's going too far. Literally.

Lesson from the 80s: When feeling the parenting strain, ask yourself WWCD? What Would Clark Do?

3 MEN AND A BABY: 1987

Three fast-living, rich, carefree bachelors get thrown in the parenting deep end when a baby turns up on their doorstep. The back-story about the heroin smugglers is best forgotten.

For all the slapstick, one-liners and *ahem* drug-smuggling in *3 Men* there are moments of poignant insight and "real" moments about the gritty side of parenting, perhaps as good as any movie about the experience has ever portrayed.

Firstly, these three guys are asses. But all men are asses. If I was single, incredibly rich, and lived with two of my best friends in a ridiculous apartment in Manhattan with a string of high-haired vixens on a revolving door/bed rotation in the hedonistic 1980s, I would be the biggest ass alive.

But here's the lesson, good and early. You can use all that ass stuff to good effect when you become a parent. Late on in the film (actually, in the much-talked about scene where the supposed "ghost" sighting takes place,) the actual baby-daddy Jack (Ted Danson) is lamenting that he's a screw-up. "You were a screw-up," says his mother (Celeste Holme) "Now you're a father." While she's right, she's wrong.

Right at the start of the movie, Peter (Tom Selleck) and Michael (Steve Guttenberg) struggle – with hilarious results – as they deal with baby Mary for the first time. "I don't know anything about babies," says Michael. "Neither do I!" says Peter. And yet, Peter figures out the bare bones within minutes; baby needs food and some diapers. "It can't be that difficult," he says. "Just feed it and it will shut up." Thus endeth the lesson.

And Michael, a creative cartoon strip artist, falls flat in his efforts to entertain Mary but keeps on trying and trying, even when his trump card of a fluffy tiger puppet falls flat.

Gentlemen, you are already well on the way.

In between scenes of the two guys (pre-Jack's arrival) nodding off to sleep, securing a bottle in Mary's mouth and rushing to close the windows in the early hours of the morning to keep the noise of the passing sirens out, we see Peter in particular start to shine. He figures out very early on that you can read anything to a baby – they don't understand the words anyway – but the singsong tone is key. Thus, he gets to be a screw-up and read a sports magazine while he should be putting the baby to sleep, and be a father by reading a "bedtime" story to his ward *at the same time*. Put that in your pipe, Jack's mom.

When Jack does get back and takes on the daddy role with gusto amid his frustration, he too uses what he knows to make things work. He's an actor. He improvises. He puts on funny voices. He does triple-duty by taking a shower, bathing the baby and keeping her entertained *at the same time*. Mom would be so proud.

The other big truth is that everyone will have advice for you, whether they are childless uncles, well-meaning friends, or mothers-of-four. As well as the shelf-stacker in the supermarket (who is actually on the money with some of the stuff she says) and the cab driver, even the narcotics cop chips in with his little old wives tale about a mythical comparison between a baby eating well and growing up confident. Brace yourself for all kinds of crap, laced with best intentions.

Sigh... and if the drug dealing back-story teaches us anything it's that it doesn't take a clichéd mobster threatening your child to make you love them more. And a doodle-laden diaper at the bottom of the doodle-diaper pail is a great place to hide heroin.

Lesson from the 80s: If these three yahoos can not only handle a baby but flourish in their role as surrogate dads, you will have no problem. You know this by now, but let me reemphasize with the help of Peter, Michael and Jack – you know more than you think you know about babies and the thing that should work best will sometimes be the biggest flop. Get. Over. It. And for those of you that think you need to leave the big city to raise a kid properly, don't just walk out on the best resource there is – the city itself – without considering the trade-off.

IRRECONCILABLE DIFFERENCES: 1984

A nine-year-old Californian girl takes her parents to court to emancipate herself. Through the power of flashback we see how her once happy, passionate parents became a couple of jerks as they got more successful in their careers at the expense of their home lives.

There are redeeming qualities to this underwhelming movie aside from the obviously impressive sight of a 26-year-old Sharon Stone's firm and fruity bosoms.

How this movie was ever really considered a comedy is a stretch though. Even as a kid, this just wasn't funny (want to know why I liked it so much when I was 10 years old though? See the paragraph above.)

It's nothing short of traumatic to see Albert (Ryan O'Neal) and Lucy (Shelley Long) fall in love to quickly, lost in a whirlwind and lust and romance, then learn to despise each other when they both get what they think they wanted. Like the judge at the start of the court hearing, we all want to find out how they got from there to "here."

Is it the fact they became parents that drove them apart? Absolutely not. It's the fact they *stopped* being parents right around the time they stopped being civil to each other. Those early days when they confront Lucy's fiancé (the late, great David Graf in the same year he made it big as Tackleberry in *Police Academy*) with such grace and dignity and logic, while the make love with passion, laugh, compliment each other and so on and so on are a long 10 years from how they are by the time daughter Casey (Drew Barrymore) gives up on them.

Lucy's eyes are opened to the Hollywood world they are about to enter when, at a screening party, one guest tells her she has kids but "isn't into parenting right now" while their host's girlfriend says the secret of their host's marriage of 35 years (to his wife – who is not the girlfriend) is that they are never together.

For all the mansions and the cars and, in Albert's case, the hot sex with Sharon Stone, all they both really want is the romance and fun they used to have. When Blake (Stone) walks in on the couple and says: "I hope I'm not interrupting anything…" it's probably too late to be asking. Their marriage is well and truly interrupted. What Albert thought he wanted was a goo-oood time in the bedroom to go with his new found uber-confidence. He ends up with Blake, who is memorably described as being good to look at with nice tits, but no Scarlett O'Hara. All Lucy thought she wanted was some recognition for her work, but when she assembles her staff to tell them her book is the number one best seller in the country and everyone just awkwardly stands there, she realizes nobody else cares as much about her as…well, *she* does.

All Casey wanted was someone to listen to her.

It's easy to see, without the help of Casey's syrupy speech in court, to see that the adults are acting like children and they made Casey grow up before she was supposed to. Everyone was happier when they had a tiny apartment and gave a rat's ass about each other. By making Casey grow up so fast, they brought the court case on themselves.

Don't get me wrong - sex with Sharon Stone and a personal chef would be nice, but what's more important than your kids and your spouse?

Lesson from the 80s: Being aware of the problem is the first step to fixing it. The old clichés are true – if you don't know who your kid's best friend at school is, you really ought to stop doing whatever it is you're doing and readjust your priorities. Not that it's very likely your kids will take you to court (unless it's on T.V. with *Judge Judy* presiding and they're short of cash.)

DIRTY DANCING: 1987

"Baby" grows up on a family vacation in 1963 when she meets Johnny, a bad boy dance instructor. Her relationship with her father is stretched as she disappoints him, but everyone learns a lesson against a backdrop (and the music) of one of the most tumultuous years in American history.

Dirty Dancing has two lessons for parents. One is about being a good dad. Dr. Jake (Jerry Orbach) is in that class of '80s dads that instantly inspire without digging too deep. The second is more to do with your kids, and letting them be kids, but knowing that one day, all of a sudden, they won't be your little boy or girl any more.

In the opening monologue, Baby (Jennifer Grey, typed with a wistful sigh) bemoans the fact she "never thought she would find a guy as great" as her dad. And for all his faults, he really is a great guy. He has John Hughes parental qualities in the way he finds time for his kids and treats his wife as an equal. Set as it is in the summer after Martin Luther King's "I Have A Dream" speech but before Kennedy's assassination, Dr. Jake makes clear his abhorrence to the "dogs in Birmingham", a reference to the segregation protests in Alabama. After Baby is paired up with the boss's son Neil (Lonny Prince) he is happy to let them go off together and do teenage stuff, which proves he trusts his daughter to have a good time – but not *too* good a time. He even named his daughter Frances after Frances Perkins, the first woman in the cabinet. He has high hopes for her in giving her (as Johnny points out later on) such a "grown-up" name.

Then there's the huge telltale sign when Baby comes to him for money – the significant amount of $250 in 1963 – but can't tell him why. He gives it up, again happy to trust the daughter that has never let him down. Naïve? Maybe. But Baby, for all her dirty "dancing" she does with Johnny later on, is hardly doing anything she wouldn't have been doing with Neil if she had gone down that path. Presumably with daddy's blessing, or at least his don't-ask-don't-tell semi-blessing.

So, a great guy, right?

Well... he has his hang-ups. As a doctor, he shows his excellent bedside manner with Penny in the aftermath of her messy operation. But he can't bring himself to even talk to Johnny when he assumes it was he that got Penny in trouble. All he sees is what so many women at the camp see – a bad boy cashing in on the opportunity to sleep around each and every summer, and to heck with who gets hurt. The twist here is, by defending Robbie, (Max Cantor) who cheats on his other daughter, Lisa (Jane Brucker) he has both guys all wrong. Well, Johnny does sleep around, but at the expense of his own self-esteem. Robbie does it because he's a douche bag.

Of course, Baby calls her dad to task in another scene that echoes so many John Hughes clashes. And she's pretty scathing in letting him have it. "There are a lot of things about me that aren't what you thought..." Nothing like telling a dad he was wrong about you to kick him in the gut. "You told me to change the world..." but on his terms, not hers. The whole scene reminds me of *Some Kind Of Wonderful* when Keith delivers a similar speech to his dad about not wanting to go to college while saying he's not stupid. Dr. Jake trusts Baby, but not when it comes to her being herself. I get the impression he may well of pushed the idea of the Peace Corps at some point, and she shrugged and thought "why not?"

Which comes back to the second point in *DD* – that innocence lost doesn't necessary make a child change for the worse. If Dr. Jake had got to know Johnny (Patrick Swayze) a little better, he would have found a well-rounded guy with morals, values and drive – and he might have even liked him. Baby is drawn to him because… well, who wouldn't be? Dude is cool. But after a summer with him, she emerges a confident, savvy woman. She starts out giddy after dancing with Johnny for the first time. By the end of their three weeks, she might feel enamored still, but she's long past the giddy stage when it comes to dealing with the opposite sex. She's so totally lost when she navigates through the room of dirty dancers, but she's grown up enough to see she's in a position to help a fellow human being.

Equally telling is when Penny (Cynthia Rhodes) tells Baby to get back to her playpen. That's all Penny wants to do herself! Her mom kicked her out when she was 16 and she grew up fast, became a Rockette, and finds herself knocked up and soon to be a single mom with no job. Innocence, once lost, never comes back. Too bad for Penny.

This three weeks was the making of Baby, simply because it reinforced and amplified the qualities she already had. Did she change after losing her innocence? Certainly, but not from white to black. That's significant. As a child, she wasn't scared of anything. As a woman, she still isn't.

The ending leaves a lot of unanswered questions. Do Baby and Johnny stay together? Does Dr. Jake forgive his daughter without reservation after admitting he was wrong to Johnny? What becomes of Lisa after learning the hard way that guys are douche bags?

Whatever happened, parent and child went through a lot together and emerged with plenty to think about. Parenthood is life, squared. When you become a parent, life changes. But as Baby proves, change can be good. And being a parent is a lot of things, but it isn't easy. You are tested daily and learning the job on the fly.

As a parent, pride in your children comes pretty naturally, and you won't need to be reminded that they don't belong in a corner. But remind yourself from time to time that you, as a parent, don't belong in the corner either. Take the spotlight, dance like nobody is watching, and look wonderful out there.

Lesson from the 80s: Kids will pick up on your inconsistencies as a parent, but we're all human – including your kids themselves of course. Also accept that things change, always and sometimes forever. If you had turned out exactly how your parents wanted you to, would you be happy? Would they?

Oh, and nobody puts Baby in the corner. That includes you.

"You're still here? It's over. Go home. Go!"

Re-watching these movies (in some cases for the hundredth time) while my kids were asleep or at pre-school came at the expense of doing the laundry, making dinner, cleaning up, and even showering - all I the name of research. For all of that, I offer a belated apology to Gwen, Penny and Patrick.

That isn't to say watching some of these movies came without an emotional toll. It still gets me anxious watching Cameron kicking dents in his dad's Ferrari in *Ferris Bueller's Day Off,* for example, and while watching *Beetlejuice* I got vivid flashbacks to a movie theater in Harrow, North London, and some mutual teenage fumbling with a female friend on a Sunday afternoon in the summer of 1988.

Of course, this book is meant to be tongue-in-cheek, but the lessons it tries to pass on are for real. Be reassured that you can be a good parent, and that you already have a selection of tools – a veritable Swiss Army Knife of on-hand solutions – to every problem that comes up with newborns through teens because you've been there, done that.

The whole idea from this book came from Darth Vader, and that should offer hope to any parent- or expectant parent. He's not cut out to be a dad, but I really think he had his son's best interests at heart by trying to recruit Luke to the Dark Side. A lesser dad wouldn't have behaved with such passion. Dude is half-machine, half-lunatic and just so angry at everything, and yet when his son turns up in *Return Of The Jedi* he gets all wistful and, inevitably does the right thing.

The same goes for the majority of the parents in John Hughes movies. They are inherently the villains of the piece, but by the end, their eyes have been opened and they really aren't so bad. And you aren't either.

On that note, I have to extend my thanks to my own mum and dad (John Hughes couldn't have made them up); my reading crew for their words of wisdom as both fellow children of the '80s and outstanding parents; Paul Imrie; Jen Singer; Simon

Ricketts, for being my unofficial editor; and James Hampton for being Teen Wolf's dad (and a gentleman.)

Adam Keeble is a father of two, originally from London, England. A journalist for more than 15 years, he has been published in a variety of regional newspapers and magazines. He now lives in New Jersey.

Made in the USA
Lexington, KY
16 December 2009